The Rain Forest Storybook

Traditional Stories from the Original Forest Peoples of South America, Africa and South-East Asia

Rosalind Kerven

CAMBRIDGE
UNIVERSITY PRESS

Published by the Press Syndicate of the University of Cambridge
The Pitt Building, Trumpington Street, Cambridge CB2 1RP
40 West 20th Street, New York, NY 10011-4211, USA
10 Stamford Road, Oakleigh, Melbourne 3166, Australia

© Cambridge University Press 1994

First published 1994

Printed in Great Britain at the University Press, Cambridge

A catalogue record for this book is available from the British Library

Library of Congress cataloguing in publication data
The rain forest storybook: traditional stories from the original forest peoples of South America,
Africa and South-east Asia / [compiled by] Rosalind Kerven.
    p.   cm.
Summary: A collection of folktales from various peoples living in rain forests around the world.
Each group of stories is introduced with information about the lives and current conditions of the
tellers of these stories.
    1. Tales – South America. 2. Tales – Africa, Southern. 3. Tales – Asia, Southeastern. [1. Folklore –
South America. 2. Folklore – Africa, Southern. 3. Folklore – Asia, Southeastern.] I. Kerven, Rosalind.
PZ8.1.R1274   1994
398.2 – dc20   93–36794   CIP

ISBN 0 521 43502 1 hardback
ISBN 0 521 43533 1 paperback

Text and cover illustrations by Rodney Sutton

Other traditional story collections by Rosalind Kerven

In the Court of the Jade Emperor: Stories from Old China
Earth Magic, Sky Magic: North American Indian Stories
King Leopard's Gift and other Animal Legends
The Tree in the Moon and other Legends of Plants and Trees
Legends of the Animal World
The Slaying of the Dragon: Tales of the Hindu Gods
The Woman Who Went to Fairyland – A Welsh Folktale

Acknowledgements

I would like to thank the following for supplying material and guidance during my research:
Survival International; The British Museum Department of Ethnography Library; Folklore Society
Library; The Horniman Museum Library; Institute of Latin American Studies Library; School of
Oriental and African Studies Library; Northumberland County Library; Embassy of Colombia;
Embassy of Ecuador; Embassy of the Republic of Indonesia; Malaysian High Commission; Betsy
King.

Survival International works with indigenous peoples of the rain forests, and other tribal peoples,
throughout the world. It helps them protect their lands, their environments and their ways of life, and
supports them in deciding their own futures. Their address is: Survival International, 310 Edgware Road,
London W2 1DY, United Kingdom.

VN

Contents

*The names shown in **bold italics** are tribal or other ethnic groups; the location is in *italics*.

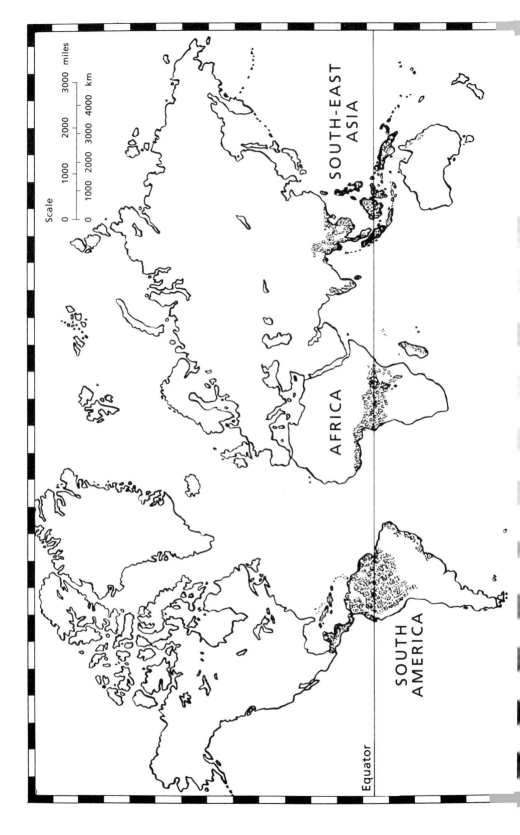

Scale

0	1000	2000	3000	miles	
0	1000	2000	3000	4000	km

SOUTH-EAST
ASIA

AFRICA

SOUTH
AMERICA

Equator

About This Book

The world's last rain forests sprawl in a thick green belt across the tropics: truly rich and marvellous places. They contain at least 2 million different plant and animal species. They play a vital part in the web of life, affecting weather patterns, water levels and even the shape of the land. Yet every year, an area nearly as big as England is destroyed for ever.

Some forests are cut down to 'harvest' their exotic timbers. Others are destroyed, then converted to farmland. Yet others are flooded by the building of huge dams to generate hydro-electricity; or carved up and polluted by mines.

As the trees die and disappear, so do their inhabitants. For though many outsiders imagine the rain forests to be empty wildernesses, millions of people have long regarded them as 'home'.

There are hundreds of different indigenous rain forest peoples scattered across the world, and each follows a unique way of life. However, many have certain things in common. In the past, these have lived in small, simple *tribal* societies that were virtually self-sufficient, finding or making everything they needed within their own patch of forest. They lived by gathering wild vegetables and fruits, or growing them in their gardens; and by hunting wild creatures for meat.

Like all societies, these have both their good and their bad points. But in one respect they have tended to be wiser than some others: generally they have lived close to nature, respecting its rhythms, and taking care not to destroy the natural environment upon which they depend.

Today, some of these tribal peoples still live in their own way. But for most of them, their unique lifestyles and beliefs – even their very existence – are being threatened by the same outsiders who come to destroy their forests.

These outsiders bring new illnesses which can prove deadly to the forest peoples, and they often criticise and ridicule tribal cultures and beliefs. Loggers, farmers and miners transform and pollute such large areas of forest land that the tribal peoples can no longer find or harvest their usual foods. Some governments encourage outsiders to seize tribal peoples' land: they station soldiers in the forests, and send officials to force the inhabitants to change suddenly to a totally alien modern lifestyle. Many of the original forest people have been brutally murdered.

However, very recently, the outlook for forest peoples has begun to look a little more hopeful. The international 'Green' movement has encouraged supporters in far away places to campaign to save the rain forests: in the process they have come to admire the people who live in them. At the same time, human rights campaigners have shocked the world with news of how the forest peoples have been abused. In some places Green campaigners and tribal peoples are now working together in their efforts to save the forests.

It is a slow and difficult struggle. Most of the countries which contain rain forests are relatively poor. Their governments resent being told how to manage their affairs by campaigners from distant rich countries – which have already destroyed most of their own natural forests. These governments insist that it is vital to clear some of their trees to enable their ever-increasing numbers of poor people to grow more food, and develop industries to give them a better standard of living. Moreover, they desperately need to sell their valuable forest timbers, and minerals from the forest mines, because they owe the rich countries a lot of money which they must pay back. Against this background, they tend to regard the forest peoples as a handful of awkward and hopelessly old-fashioned obstacles, who should be prepared to move and get 'civilised' for the good of the wider community.

This book contains a sample of the countless myths, legends and folk-tales told by some of the original inhabitants of the largest remaining rain forests. Many of these stories are very old. The forest peoples have passed them down from one generation to the next by word of mouth. Mostly they have only been formally collected and written down in the last hundred years, by visiting anthropologists (people who study small-scale societies), Christian missionaries, foreign government officials, and interested travellers.

Some may have deeper meanings that we cannot understand. Some have been re-spun as the story-tellers make sense of the outside world that is creeping in on their territory. Others are more recent and attempt to explain the frightening changes which have suddenly been thrown at the people.

They are all intriguing; many are haunting, some are amusing; each is touched by a sense of the common humanity which we share with these distant peoples. Also each seems to say something worth listening to about how human beings can relate to the rain forests and to the wider natural world.

Above all, they are the human voice behind one of the major environmental tragedies of our time.

The Forest Peoples of South America

2 Existing rain forests in South America.

*'The forest exists – it has energy and breathes, spirits exist in the
mountains and rivers and plants. I think you should dream of the planet,
because it has a heart and breathes.'*
Davi, spokesperson of the Yanomami people

The River Amazon is 3,900 miles long (6,280 kilometres). It has
over a thousand tributaries and contains a fifth of all the Earth's
fresh water. Around – and far beyond – its banks, stretching over
2.3 million square miles (6 million square kilometres) grows the
largest surviving expanse of tropical rain forest in the world.

The Amazonian rain forest is spread over nine countries: Bolivia,
Brazil, Colombia, Ecuador, French Guiana, Guyana, Peru, Surinam
and Venezuela. Its numerous wild creatures include jaguars,
pumas, alligators, giant water-snakes and about half the world
total of bird species.

The tribal peoples who live in the Amazonian rain forest are
generally all known as 'Indians'. (This name was given to all the
original inhabitants of the Americas by European explorers,
because when they first reached the continents, they mistakenly
believed they were in India.) There are a great number of different
tribes, each with its own name and language, its own unique way
of doing things, its own laws, religion and stories.

In the past, most of these peoples lived by growing crops in their
forest gardens; by hunting animals and birds with bows and poison-
tipped arrows, spears or blowpipes; by fishing; and by gathering
wild fruits and vegetables. They wove cloth and baskets and made
pottery and bark-cloth. They wore few clothes, but were very
skilled at making beautiful ornaments and painting their bodies
with elaborate designs. They also made canoes from hollowed-out
trees, for travel by river was the quickest and easiest way of
getting around.

Some tribes were nomadic (constantly moving about) and built
only very simple huts. But among the more settled peoples, a
typical village would contain large houses with wooden frames
and thatched roofs in which a number of families lived. Everyone
slept in hammocks made of twine, cotton or bark. The cooking
fires were kept burning all the time.

Among the most important people in any community were the
'shamans' or religious leaders. Usually men, they could communicate

with supernatural spirits, heal the sick and advise on the future. They also kept alive their people's most important sacred stories. Amazonian religion was centred mainly on a belief in nature spirits. Some animals were held to have special magical links with the people, or to be their spiritual ancestors. Jaguars especially carried strong mystical powers.

For hundreds of years, the Amazonian Indians have suffered appallingly at the hands of European incomers. Millions of people have been deliberately and viciously killed as if they were insignificant vermin; governments have allowed their murderers to escape without punishment; and a great many tribes have been completely wiped out. Others have been enslaved; they have seen their land stolen, their trees destroyed and their rivers polluted. Their suffering continues today.

However, very recently the future has begun to look a little more hopeful.

The Yanomami of Brazil and Venezuela are the largest surviving Amazonian tribe still following their own way of life. In 1990 they numbered about 20,000 people, living in an area almost as big as Switzerland. They have had many troubles. In recent years the Brazilian government has organised a road building programme through their forest; also thousands of small-scale gold miners and other outsiders have invaded their land; and more stretches of forest have been destroyed to build 100 airstrips to fly in supplies. The newcomers have brought in new deadly diseases as well as social problems such as alcoholism.

The Yanomami's plight was brought to world attention by international rain forest and human rights campaigners. Many outraged supporters in far away countries began to protest about how they and other forest peoples were being treated.

As a result, in 1991 the government of Venezuela made their part of the Yanomami's land into a 'biosphere reserve'. Outsiders are not allowed to settle in or develop it: they are not even allowed to visit it without a permit. The Yanomami and their neighbours the Yekuana tribe are being encouraged to continue their traditions and are being given special medical help. Shortly after this the government of Brazil also set aside a special 'Yanomami Park', recognising the tribe's legal right to occupy their traditional lands. Although both governments still face a difficult task in forcing aggressive outsiders to leave Yanomami land, these are major victories for the rights of the original rain forest people.

Similar small changes for the better have followed elsewhere. For example the governments of Colombia and Bolivia have also recently granted tribal peoples legal rights over sizeable areas of rain forest. Moreover, the Colombian government has stated its belief that returning land to the tribal peoples who understand how to look after it is the best way of preserving the rain forest.

Meanwhile, some Amazonian peoples have become increasingly expert at using modern, non-violent methods to protect themselves. One of their greatest victories was in 1989. The Brazilian government had planned to build a huge hydro-electric dam on the Xingu River. This would have flooded a vast area of rain forest and destroyed many tribal peoples' homes. Leaders of the Kayapo people responded by travelling to see political and financial leaders in many countries to explain the threat to the environment and the people. They then organised a mass protest meeting attended by hundreds of forest people from 40 different local tribes, which was publicised by newspapers and television throughout the world. They succeeded in stopping the dam from being built.

Most (though not all) Amazonian peoples have now had considerable contact with 'civilised' outsiders. Even those groups which have managed to preserve their traditional cultures recognise the need to become part of the wider national and global communities if they are to be successful in saving both their own people and their forest. They make good use of money which is sent to them by sympathetic campaigners overseas, spending it for example on medicines and flying doctors; and on educating their leaders to be literate, and to understand subjects like law so that they can continue to protect their rights in the future. They are also learning that modern technology can help them in their own way; for example, the Kayapo have begun to record some of their ceremonies on video, in order to ensure that their traditions are kept alive for future generations.

Jaguar-Man
Desana, Colombia

Jaguar: take care, hide yourself when his footfalls come near.

Jaguar: he is the master − of thunder, of fire; moon-brother, sun-brother, master of the caves and mountains, chief of all the animals . . .

Jaguar: he goes where he will, does what he wants; friend or enemy, he chooses to please himself. Love him, fear him, always respect him . . .

Listen: more mysteries. *There are men in this village who can transform themselves into jaguars.* The shamans, the wise men, the mystery men: the ones who can make their minds fly freely to run with the spirits, and come back again.

Jaguar: is he man or spirit, cat or shaman? Who can tell, when he passes so softly, softly through the shadows?

There was a man once lived here, who hadn't been married long before there were terrible arguments; and then his wife left him. He felt lonely and wretched after that. There was no one to cook the meat he brought home, no one to mend his hammock, no one to bear him children. The other men laughed at him, the women shook their heads and gossiped as he went past. He was an outcast. After a few days of this, he wandered away all alone, off the trails, into the deepest part of the forest. Everyone thought he was probably gone for good.

But a year later he came back − and his wife was with him again.

This time there was no arguing between them: instead they clung to each other and there was a strange wildness in their eyes.

'Where have you been?' everyone asked them. 'What has happened to you?' But they always shook their heads. 'If we tell you the truth,' said the wife, 'you will never believe us.'

Time passed. Then one night a group of us were gathered at someone's hearth in the *maloca*, the village house, chatting and swapping stories. The talk turned to jaguars, to transformations, to magic. Everyone was getting sleepy, light-headed: the night was at its blackest. Out of the shadows a low voice said:

'We've seen one.' It was the man who had gone missing.

'Me and her. We met a jaguar-man.'

No one else spoke. The voice went on:

'It was that time last year when I walked off. I went on and on, deep into the trees, for hours, far away from any place I'd been to before. I walked for five days. I was nowhere near any village. Then suddenly I met a stranger. This man, he wore no belt or body-paint, no beads or feathers, nothing. But over his shoulder he carried a basket; and in the basket was the skin of a jaguar. He came right up to me, and his presence made me shiver.

' "Where are you going?" the stranger asked.

' "I am going to lose myself in the forest," I replied, "because my wife doesn't love me."

' "Oh-oh!" cried the stranger "We can't have that!" Then he roared, deep in his throat. "Tell me about her: who she is and where she is to be found."

'I told him everything. "I will fetch her back for you," he said. Then he went bounding off, leaving me feeling dazed and terrified at the foot of a tree.'

The man fell silent after that. A log shifted in the thick night ashes of the cooking fire. After a few moments, his wife's voice took up the story.

'I was taking my pot down to the river to fetch some water,' said she. 'Suddenly a huge black jaguar leaped out of the bushes and seized me in his mouth! I thought it was my end – but he didn't eat me. Instead he carried me, gently, gently, cradled in his teeth, deep into the thickest part of the forest. At last we came to the spot where my husband was waiting. The jaguar dropped me on the ground. Then he shed his skin just like a snake does – and turned himself into a man! "I forbid you to leave your husband ever again!" he roared. His eyes were hard and yellow, like flames; sparks hissed and spat out of his mouth as he spoke. I feared his man-shape much more than his jaguar-shape. I took my husband's hand and promised to obey.

'After that, the jaguar-man softened a little. "Come with me," he said. "I shall take you to my house in the western headwaters." He set off then, turning, always turning to watch us.

Well, the two of us were stuck in this together now: it helped to make us friends. We clung to each other and went after him.

'When night fell, we stopped and made a fire. My husband caught a small monkey: we cooked and ate it, but the jaguar-man would eat nothing. Then we all lay down and went to sleep.

'When we woke next morning, he had turned back into a huge black jaguar. He was lying right beside us. His claws were out, and when he snored, his mouth opened a little, showing his teeth.

'The two of us started to whisper, trying to work out a way to escape. But the jaguar kept twitching his ears.

' "I am listening!" he growled at us. "I hear everything you say." Then he stretched, stood up and he was a man again. He kept saying, "Stay with me, follow me, don't be afraid." His voice was strangely soft when he said it. We had no choice but to keep on going after him.'

'At last we came to a huge, painted *maloca*. He was in his jaguar-shape now: black, huge, powerful. "Hold tightly to my tail," he said. We did this. The door opened before him and he led us in.

'Inside the house, there were many, many other jaguars. They seemed to be gathered there for a festival. Some were black, like him; others were marked and spotted.

'They danced and sang, these creatures; they passed around bowl after bowl overflowing with food and drink. When they came to *our* jaguar they all bowed and offered him the best of everything.

'For he was no ordinary creature, he who had taken us into his power: he was their chief!

'At last everything was finished. He took us back through the forest. He brought us home here. "That party was your proper wedding feast," he said. "You married under my eyes, and my bond may never be broken."

'So there, at last, is our story.'

No, of course there is no knowing how much of this is true. But I tell you, there were shamans listening that night, and they believed it. Besides, that man and that woman, who were once so full of hate and anger, since their lost year in the forest, they have always lived together in peace.

Gifts from the River

Waiwai, Brazil and Guyana

So – you like the way we decorate ourselves, do you? Don't be shy, come closer, take a proper look. Oh yes, I'm sure you must have heard that we Waiwai wear the finest beads and feathers in all of the Amazon forest!

I'll tell you why they're so fine: they were a gift from the Anaconda-People. What! You haven't heard of them? I can see you have a lot of learning to do, my friend.

You know what an anaconda is, of course? It's the giant water-snake that lives in our rivers. Huge things, they are – some are as long as five men laid end-to-end.

Now then, you must understand that the Anaconda-People are our relations. They are our ancestors. Yes, this is quite true. We worship them; but we are a little afraid of them as well.

There was once a Waiwai girl who got left behind. Everyone else had gone off to the next village for a festival; but this girl was not allowed to go. The reason was this: she had reached that wonderful, dangerous stage of life when she was turning from an innocent child into a beautiful young woman; and such girls must be shut away from everyone else for two whole moons. It keeps them safe, you see, while they learn all the things a woman needs to know.

This girl remembered how all her older sisters, cousins and friends had once been shut away too; but that did not stop her from feeling bad. The next village was not far away: day and night she could hear the noise of her friends' singing and merry-making drifting over the trees. She was seething with frustration, stuck at home in a dark hut, with only a sour old grandmother to keep her company.

Now one morning, this old woman who was guarding her, looking after her, she needed some water. So, seeing they were all alone, she let the girl out of her hut and sent her down to the river to fetch it.

'Go straight there,' she said, 'do the job as quickly as you can, and then bring the water straight back here to me. And just you listen, girl: whatever you do, *don't look into the middle of the river.* For that is where the Anaconda-People like to swim and play. If they see a girl-who-is-becoming-a-woman like you, daring to watch them, you can be sure – *they will run straight out to get you!*'

'Yes Grandmother,' said the girl politely. But inside her head she was thinking, 'Silly old woman! She's just making up childish stories to keep me shut up. I bet these so-called Anaconda-People are just ordinary water-snakes, no different from any of the other creatures in the forest.'

So she hurried down to the river; and when she reached the bank, she stopped and stared, straight out into the middle.

At that very moment the brown water began to froth and bubble. Then the surface broke – and out burst a mass of huge, writhing snakes! The foolish girl, she just went on staring and staring; and as she watched, one by one, the anacondas shed their skins. Out of each skin stepped a tall, strong man or woman!

While this was happening, a terrible noise broke out: whistling, shrieking and calling. All around the mass of Anaconda-People, other water creatures were also rising from the river and changing into people. There were small fish, big fish, tiger-fish, electric eels and sting-rays.

As soon as they were all transformed, the River-People began to walk. They came straight across the river, towards the bank where the girl stood. At first, she couldn't move at all. She was transfixed with wonder and terror.

Closer and closer they came. What did they want of her? They did not look fierce or violent. No, instead they were all smiling and holding out their arms in welcome. All at once, she realised what was going on. They wanted to take her away with them, down, down to the deep, dark bottom of the river. And there they would probably make her marry an Anaconda-Man!

With that thought, the girl came suddenly to her senses. She had to get away! She screamed, she turned and ran – running, running, back up the path, as fast as ever she could.

Back in the hut, the sour old woman was waiting for her.

'Grandmother, Grandmother!' shrieked the poor girl, 'I've seen them – I've seen the Anaconda-People! It was just as you warned me: they're coming to get me! Help, oh help me please!'

'Why, you good-for-nothing little fool!' scolded the old woman. 'Why don't you obey your elders, as you have been taught to, since the very day that you were born? Yes, indeed, they are coming to get you. And listen to this, wretch: they will scent you out wherever you hide. Anyway, you don't deserve to escape!'

At this, the girl began to cry so bitterly that pity stirred in the old woman's shrivelled-up heart. 'Oh, come then,' said she, 'let's see what we can do for you. Get over here and sit down.'

The girl sat. When she was comfortable, the old woman picked up an enormous basket and placed it right over her. Now she was completely hidden.

No sooner was this done, than the Anaconda-People arrived at the hut. The other Fish-People – hundreds of them – were thronging around them. They were all strong and beautiful to look at, but they smelled of river water, and their skins were scaly and covered in the mottled patterns of their kind. Under the basket, the girl shivered and shuddered.

But the Anaconda-People and their followers did not come in. They stayed outside. They began to dance. First they danced right round the house in a slow ring. Then they stood still and stamped the ground: thud-thud-thud, like this, in a slow rhythm, as if they were at a feast, waiting, waiting for the drinking bowl to be passed round. But here it was no drink they wanted, oh no: here they were waiting, waiting for the girl who was to be their bride!

Through the holes in the basket, the girl was peering out and watching them. She could see them in a circle, the River-Men, River-Women, with their strange skins, all bright with ornaments that shimmered and dazzled and swayed as they danced.

'*Where's the girl, Grandmother?*' they chanted.
'*Where's the girl,*
where's the girl,
Grandmother – where's the girl?'

Meanwhile, the old woman was stoking up the fire. Soon the flames burned brightly, strongly. Then she took a handful of pepper and flung it on top. At once the fire flared up: sizzling and giving off thick, foul-smelling smoke.

'Get away with you!' the old woman shrieked back at them. 'There's no girl here. There's only me – and I'm no use as a bride to anyone!'

But the River-People shouted back at her: 'Don't try fooling us, Grandmother!' Then their dance grew faster, giddier; and they began to sing:

'*Ya ra ki ki yenna,*
Ya ra ki ki yenna.'

As they sang, a giant armadillo came out from the forest. It went to the river bank and began to dig a tunnel. This tunnel started at the river and it ran under the earth, straight to the girl's hut. Very soon where she crouched, river water began to seep under the floor, until it grew soft and damp. Then the water came properly bubbling up and trickled over the girl's feet.

But she stayed in her hiding place.

Night fell. The moon moved across the sky. The River-People stayed there, dancing and singing. Inside the hut, water from the armadillo's tunnel began to rise slowly but steadily up the walls.

Still the girl did not come out.

At last it was dawn again. The Anaconda-People and the other River-People were tired. They stopped singing, they stopped dancing.

Inside the wet hut, under her basket, the girl heard a terrific commotion. There was rattling and thumping. People climbed up onto the roof. She was terrified: they would jump down, they would rush in, they would take her away by force!

But the next thing she knew was silence. Then the old woman was calling her: 'They've gone away, girl. But thanks to them – no, thanks to *you* – we are about to be flooded. Quick – come out of there – run – follow me!'

So the two of them hurried away, away from the rising water. They ran down a trail and into the forest. There they met the rest of the villagers, who were on their way back from the festival, laughing and happy.

But they soon put aside their laughter when they heard what had happened! They were angry, I can tell you! The village headman himself took the girl aside and you can be sure he gave her a talking to:

'This is what happens when you break the laws, fool of a girl! This is what happens when you do things that the wise ones of long ago taught us are forbidden!'

Meanwhile, some men went back to the village to see what had happened. All the houses were under water, their gardens were under water, everything was ruined.

And yet . . . these men, they came back carrying armfuls of extraordinary things. There were arm-bands, leg-bands, criss-crossing body-bands, all made of wonderful, glistening, translucent beads. There were hair-tubes of beads and feathers, each one as long as a man's back. There were more beautiful feathers too, feathers fashioned to go on the chin, feathers for the nose, feathers to wear in the corner of the mouth. Each thing was brilliantly coloured, iridescent, perfect.

The Anaconda-People had put all these things on the roof of the hut, you see, so that they would be safe from the flood water. That was the noise the girl heard right at the end. They had meant them as bride-gifts, to be given in exchange for the girl. Even though she would not go with them to get married under the water, still they left their gifts for us, to show there was no bad feeling. For whatever happens, the Anaconda-People are more than in-laws: they are our ancestors, our relations, our kin.

I'm not sure what happened to the girl. Maybe they sent her away into the forest for shame; or maybe instead they honoured her for the gifts she unwittingly brought them.

For ever since then, we've been wearing beads and feathers in the style that the Anaconda-People showed us. Go on, admire them some more! No tribe has ever had a better gift from the river.

Bumblebee Spat

Yanomami, Brazil and Venezuela

It was long, long ago. There was a village where the people did everything wrong. They must have been idiots, because all day long they offended the spirits. They offended them when they went hunting, when they tended their gardens, when they brought food home, and when they cooked it to eat. They did not know the correct way to do these things, you see. They were primitive, ignorant people; and they had no shamans (no wise men, no spirit talkers) – not one – to show them the way.

Because of this, the whole of nature was angry with them. The river was angry, the hills were angry, the trees and bushes and creepers were angry. The Earth itself shook with rage, and thunder rumbled constantly across the sky.

Then, out of every shadow and corner, dark spirits came dancing. Hideous creatures they were, twisted with disgust at the stupidity of the people.

'Make it rain!' they shrieked. Then the sky cracked, and the rain spirits hurled torrents of water down onto the village.

At once the whole *yano* – the village house where everyone lived – was completely washed away: gone, finished. The people who lived in it were swept away too. But they did not drown.

Before their eyes, as they swirled around in the flood water, they saw the angry spirits twist and transform themselves. Now they were gigantic otters – each one as big as a tree! No, no, now they were night-black alligators: their teeth snapped and gnashed, eager to slice each person into shreds!

A fury of water; a fury of teeth. And then . . . a fury of silence.

Soon all that remained of these poor, foolish people was their blood.

This blood, it turned the surface of the water into pink foam. The foam drifted softly. It drifted and drifted out to sea, on and on, until it came to a beach. This beach was far, far away. It was right at the very edge of the world.

Here, at the end of everything, lived Bumblebee. He was the first bee and he had power, marvellous power.

When the pink foam came to him, Bumblebee drank it up: he swallowed it. Then he brought it back up again and held it in his mouth. He let his breath dance sweetly through it. He whispered over it: strange words, magic words, strong words.

Then he spat the foam out again and bits of it flew to every corner of the world.

The foam became people: not Yanomami like us, but foreigners like you. The seeds of all peoples in every place who are not Yanomami, they were sown long ago from that foam that Bumblebee transformed.

Because of this, we know that all peoples are related, all races are one race; and every tribe, every nation is born from the foam of those first Yanomami.

Us and You

Ufaina, Colombia

Yurupari, he is a god. He lives far away across the river, far beyond the rapids.

It was long ago, back at the beginning of all things. I have seen this time in my mind's eye, using that deep inner eye that only a shaman can open. I travelled through the secret mind's door into that long ago time: this is what I saw . . .

I saw Yurupari with a basket full of gifts. He wanted to share these good things with people; for, at that time, the people had nothing. They were no better than animals: they could do the things that animals can do, but nothing more.

So he called across the river and the people came to him. Then, as now, there were many different tribes. They waded across the water to him, one tribe at a time. He greeted them as a father greets his children, and gave each tribe a different gift.

To the first tribe he gave baskets: he taught them how to make them, and how to use them. To the next tribe he gave spears, to the next bows and arrows, and to the next one hammocks.

Thus and thus, one gift after another, he shared with the forest peoples. One tribe after another, they came to him; they collected their gifts; they thanked him; they went home.

Still, still as a rock, still as a mountain, Yurupari waited. More people were coming. But these were people from another world, from the world beyond the forest. They were strangers, the ancestors of city people, *your* people.

'Welcome!' called Yurupari. 'Wade across the river to me! I have precious things to give you.'

'Why should we come to you?' your people shouted back. 'How do we know we can trust you? What can you possibly have that we might want?'

Yurupari was amused at their suspicion. 'For you . . . now let me see . . . Ah yes, I have the best gifts of all!' he said. 'I have

Thought; I have Knowledge; I have Understanding. If you come to me, I will show you how it is possible to understand everything in the world, everything in the universe!'

But your people had no trust: they stayed just where they were. They stared at the swirling river and told themselves it was too wild, too hostile, totally impossible to wade across.

'We need to make something that can carry us safely across it,' they said to each other. So they sat down and measured and muddled and made things. Thousands of years passed: but at last they had a boat. 'We're coming!' they called.

But Yurupari, he laughed at them: 'Why did you need to invent a boat to travel through the water? Fish have been doing this much more skilfully than anything you can make, right since the beginning of time.'

Your people, they think they're the greatest, cleverest tribe in the whole world: greater than the gods, even. They didn't like the way Yurupari mocked at their achievements. So straight away they got out more tools to measure and calculate. They were determined to invent something even better, much better than a boat. This thing, they decided, would stretch right over the widest part of the river in a single span, so that they could walk straight across it without getting wet. At last – a few thousand years later – they had got it right: they made a bridge.

'That's quite good,' chuckled Yurupari. 'You have made some-thing nearly as clever (but not quite) as the vines and creepers which have been growing quietly, twisting and tangling, stretching themselves over the river, ever since the beginning of time!'

At this, your people started to get into a real rage. They couldn't take all this mockery. 'All right,' they said, 'we'll show you, you stupid old forest-god! Keep your worthless gifts for your-self: we already have all the knowledge and understanding that we want anyway. Just to prove it, we'll show you how we're the only people on Earth who can *fly* across the river!'

So they went away for another few thousand years. They measured and fumbled about, until at last they had invented the aeroplane. They were pretty proud of that, oh yes!

From far away, Yurupari saw it. 'It's not bad,' he said, 'but it doesn't work anything like as well as a bird. And birds have been around since the beginning of time, you know.

'Now listen my friends: why don't you leave all your crazy little inventions alone for a while? Calm down, and just come, wade straight across the river to me. This gift I have for you – true Knowledge, true Wisdom – will prove itself far more precious than anything you can possibly make yourselves.'

But they would not come, your people. They stayed where they were, on their side of the river. There they continued to invent and fashion many machines, many gadgets. They were ingenious, these things, and yet . . . you know, each one was just a poor, hollow imitation of what already exists in nature. Even a bomb: it is only a copy of a volcano. Even a computer: it is just a poor, cold imitation of a living human mind.

Ever since then, true Knowledge, true Understanding has stayed just where it has always been. It lies way across the river from you, deep, deep in the forest, safe with Yurupari, and safe with us, the forest people.

The Old Sun

Juruna, Brazil

The Sun that shines down on Earth, he is a man you know. He lives in the sky. Every dawn he puts on his head-dress and carries light and warmth across the world until he reaches the western dusk. His head-dress is made of feathers, feathers of fire.

But this Sun, the one we know, he is not the first Sun. Once, when the world was young, there was another: his father, the old Sun. He was evil, that one. He liked to kill people. But at last he himself was killed by a great hero. This hero was a Juruna, a man of our own tribe.

I'll tell you how it happened.

The old Sun had a house, far away. Outside his house was a stone. In the middle of the stone was a hole. The hole was always full of water. It was a trap for catching things: animals – or people! Any creature that put its head inside the trap to drink would get stuck. Then the Sun would pull it out, and eat it.

One day a young man from our tribe went past the Sun's house. He didn't know about the trap. He was very thirsty, so when he saw the hole in the stone, full of water, he went straight up to it and took a drink.

And at once – *aagh!* – he was stuck!

There was nothing he could do, so he waited. The rest of the day passed, and then the night. Then it was morning again. The Sun rose and came out of his house. The first thing he did was inspect his trap. He was delighted to find a meaty young man caught inside it!

The youth was terrified. He did not know what to do, so he pretended to be dead. He lay utterly still. He did not move at all: not a limb, not a muscle. Even his heart was scarcely beating. The Sun pulled him out of the trap and threw him into his basket. He carried the basket back to his house and hung it from the branch of a tree. Then he left it there, and went on with his daily journey across the sky.

The day passed and night fell. In the darkness, the young man crept out of the basket and hid in the tree's hollow root.

The next morning the Sun went to fetch the youth. His mouth was watering at the thought of eating him. He looked in the basket and found that it was empty. He began to blaze with fury.

He looked here, he looked there. At last he found the youth, cowering deep inside the hollow. He picked up his cudgel and began to beat on the tree trunk; but he could not get the youth out. So he took a long stick, and used it to poke and prise around inside the hollow. Still he could not get the youth out: instead, he actually wedged him in so deeply that he could not even move. Even worse, the youth was wounded most terribly from the top of his head to his feet.

It was getting late. The Sun had to go, he had to set. He covered up the entrance to the hollow with a big stone. 'I'll be back for you tomorrow!' he roared. Then he went.

Now it was night. The youth lay moaning with pain. Many animals heard his cries.

They came to see who it was, what was wrong. There were monkeys, tapirs, wild pigs, agoutis and many others. They felt sorry for the youth. And they hated the old Sun, for many of their own relations had previously died in his trap.

They all wanted to help. So they started to dig, to burrow. Each animal worked and worked until it was ready to drop. Then others came to help. They worked all night until they had dug a big hole. Then they took turns to lick his wounds until they began to heal.

The young man squeezed out of the hole. He thanked the animals; he ran home.

Back in his village, he told his relations what had happened. His mother wept when she heard how he had nearly died.

Three days passed. The youth had completely recovered from his wounds. He was restless: he wanted to go out.

He knew the Sun would still be after him, so he made a disguise. He cut off all his hair and painted his body so that he looked like a monkey. Then he went into the forest and began to climb palm trees to pick some coconuts.

He hadn't been doing this for very long before the old Sun himself came passing by. The youth's disguise didn't fool him at all: the Sun scented him out straight away.

'I shall get you this time!' he roared. 'Come down!'

'All right,' the youth called back, 'but first could you just catch this bunch of coconuts?'

The Sun liked coconuts. 'Go on then,' he replied, 'throw them down.'

The youth threw them, and the Sun caught them easily.

'There's some more up here.'

'Throw them to me!' roared the Sun. 'Throw them all!'

This time the youth broke off a really huge bunch. It was so heavy, he could scarcely hold it. The Sun stood on the ground below waiting for it, with his arms stretched out wide, ready to catch it.

The youth hurled the bunch, as hard as he could. It struck the Sun full in the chest like a bolt of thunder. It killed him.

The old Sun, the cruel Sun, was dead!

But the death of a Sun means the death of everything. It means darkness and cold.

When the youth went back to his village, he found that the children were dying. Everyone else was shivering and starving It was too dark to fish or hunt, or work in the gardens, or gather wild food.

So the old Sun was dead; but he left behind a widow and three sons.

His widow said to her boys, 'One of you must take over your father's work. Which one will it be?'

The oldest one tried. He put on the fire-feather head-dress and set off across the sky. But the fire was too hot for him: he couldn't bear it. He gave up and came home before the end of the day.

Next morning, the second boy tried. He could not bear the heat either, so he gave up and came home too.

The youngest boy was the last to try. He put on the fire-feathers and managed to carry them right across the sky. The first day he did it, he walked too quickly: night came much too soon. But after that he learned to rest at the top of the sky at midday and soon he was good at it.

This new Sun, he doesn't eat people like his father did. We like him.

The Magic Canoe

Kamaiura, Brazil

There was once a man who made a canoe. It was a really fine one, fashioned out of bark from the jatoba tree.

It took him hours and hours to finish it. When at last it was done, he went home proudly to tell his wife. But she was much too busy to hear the news – for the baby they had been expecting had just that moment been born!

Now the man did what every new father should do: he stayed at home. He did not hunt or fish with the other men. He left the new canoe just where it was, out in the forest, by the river.

Many days passed. His wife and little child had settled down. It was time for him to get to work again. He couldn't wait to catch some fish from his fine new canoe. So off he went to inspect it.

But when he came to the place where he had left it – the boat had gone.

He sat down under the jatoba tree and puzzled over what had happened. He sat there for a long time.

By and by, he began to hear a strange noise: *ssshhheee*, like this, coming from the forest. The next minute, he saw something very strange too. He was no shaman, this man – yet it seemed that he was being visited by spirits!

He sat very still, waiting. He felt too shaken to stand up. The strange thing was coming closer. This spirit that he could see and hear with his own eyes and ears: it was his canoe!

The canoe had grown two legs to walk on; a mouth and two eyes, one on each side of the prow. It walked right up to him and stopped.

Not knowing what else to do, the man climbed inside. The canoe stood still, waiting. Perhaps it was waiting for instructions.

'Can you . . . can you carry me to the lagoon?' whispered the man.

At once the canoe set off briskly. It waddled on its legs, *uh-uh, uh-uh*, going exactly the way the man wanted it to. Very soon they reached the lagoon, and the canoe slid into the water.

The next moment, hundreds of fish began to jump out of the water and into the canoe, one after the other: *splat, splat, splat* and so on. The man stared in amazement. Then the canoe twisted round its prow, opened its mouth and swallowed them all up!

No sooner had it finished than more fish began to jump in. This time, however, the canoe did not touch them, but let them lie thrashing about around the man in its hollow back.

When it was quite full to the brim, the canoe turned around and paddled itself back to the bank. It dragged itself out of the water without waiting for further instructions, and walked straight back to the jatoba tree.

There it stopped, waiting again. The man climbed out; then he pulled all the fish out after him. Surely they must be meant for him!

'Thank you very much,' he said.

The canoe said not a word; but its two eyes were watching him, watching him intently.

The man patted the canoe. Then he cut some vines and knotted them into a big, strong bag. He filled the bag with the fish.

'Just you wait here,' he said to the canoe. 'I'll be back in a few days.'

He took the bag of fish and ran home to his wife. She was hungry as anything, what with nursing the baby all day and night. The fish kept them happy for many days.

The man whispered not a word to anyone about how he had caught them.

When all the fish were gone, the man went back to find the canoe again. This time he was all ready with a large basket. The canoe was not where he had left it, but very soon it appeared, just like before, waddling noisily towards him through the trees on its unnatural spindly legs, staring at him with its disconcerting eyes.

The canoe stopped and the man climbed in. Just as before, it carried him down to the lagoon and plunged into the water. Just as before, one fish after another jumped inside it. The man was really excited. He'd never have to work again! All he had to do was sit back and let the food come to him.

Without wasting any time, he started to cram the fish into his basket, one after another. Faster and faster he worked. Everything was happening just as he remembered it, only better . . .

But he had not remembered everything. He had forgotten that the canoe was really a spirit; and he had forgotten also that the first batch of fish were meant for the canoe to eat.

An angry spirit is dangerous, deadly dangerous.

When his basket was full, he sat back and suddenly such thoughts did come to him. But it was too late.

For at that moment the magic canoe turned round and opened its mouth, wide. In one gulp it swallowed up all the fish . . . and then it swallowed the man up too!

The Forest Peoples of Africa

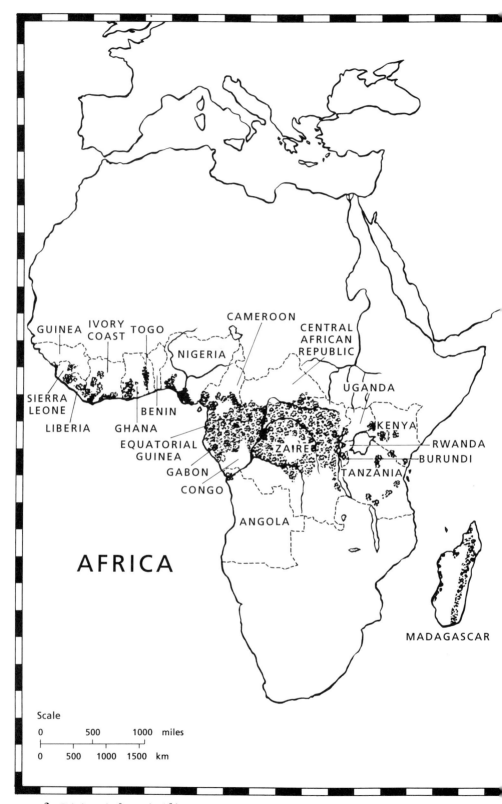

GUINEA
IVORY
COAST
TOGO
CAMEROON
CENTRAL
AFRICAN
REPUBLIC
NIGERIA
UGANDA
SIERRA
LEONE
BENIN
KENYA
LIBERIA
GHANA
RWANDA
EQUATORIAL
GUINEA
ZAIRE
BURUNDI
GABON
TANZANIA
CONGO
ANGOLA

AFRICA

MADAGASCAR

Scale

0	500	1000	miles

0	500	1000	1500	km

3 Existing rain forests in Africa.

*'The forest is a father and mother to us . . . it gives us everything we need
— food, clothing, shelter, warmth . . . and affection.'*

Moke, a Mbuti Pygmy

A vast stretch of almost untouched rain forest stretches across six
countries in the heart of Africa: Cameroon, Central African Republic,
Congo, Equatorial Guinea, Gabon and Zaire. This is the territory of
some of the Earth's most intelligent wild creatures such as gorillas,
chimpanzees and forest elephants. Zaire alone contains 409
different species of mammal and over 11,000 plant species.

Once there was another huge rain forest spread along the coast
of west Africa, spanning eight countries from Sierra Leone to
Nigeria. In the last hundred years over three-quarters of this has
been cut down. Some has disappeared to create new farms and to
supply cooking fuel for the area's rapidly growing populations.
But during the 1980s the main cause of destruction was to supply
tropical timber to Britain and other European countries.

As a result, Africa has lost a greater proportion of its rain
forests than any other continent. The European logging companies
which have already deforested west Africa are now preparing to
repeat the process in central Africa. Ninety per cent of the forest
in the Central African Republic is scheduled to be cut down, as
are large areas in Zaire, Congo, Cameroon and Gabon.

In the Middle Ages powerful kingdoms and empires flourished
in the central African rain forests. These were highly organised,
sophisticated cultures, ruled by a king or queen with the help of
court officials. They were quite different from the simple tribal
societies of other rain forests elsewhere: many of these people
specialised in particular types of work and were highly skilled.

From the 16th century onwards, these forest kingdoms
gradually lost all their power and strength. As in other parts of
Africa, one of the main causes was the slave trade, in which local
kings and chiefs sold millions of their most able people to
European traders, who then shipped them to a life of horrendous
cruelty as slaves in the newly 'discovered' Americas. Then in the
late 19th and early 20th centuries almost the whole of Africa was
conquered by European empires. Most of the present rain forest
area was controlled by Belgium, with smaller sections taken over
by France, Spain and Germany. Since the Second World War these

countries have regained their independence. However, European influence has strongly affected their cultures.

Nevertheless, in central Africa there is one 'true' rain forest tribal culture: known to outsiders as 'Pygmies'. There are thought to be about 250,000 of these people who still live as nomadic hunters and gatherers.

The Mbuti Pygmies inhabit the Ituri Forest of Zaire. They live together in small bands of between three and forty families. They have no formal leaders; 'experts' and older people are generally listened to with respect, but they make all their decisions and sort out problems by group discussion. Women and men are regarded as equals, and although they do have some separate areas of work, many tasks – including child-care – are shared.

The women's main skill is gathering wild foods including mushrooms and other edible fungi, roots, nuts, berries and caterpillars. They also build all the huts: these have a frame of saplings (cut by the men) into which are woven large leaves. They can build a whole long-lasting, twelve-hut camp within two days.

The men's main work is hunting: they catch many different animals including antelope, wild pig, monkeys and even, very rarely, elephants. Some bands hunt with bows and poisoned arrows; others work as a group, chasing animals into nets (with the women and children acting as beaters) and then killing them with spears, knives or arrows. The men are also expert at collect-ing wild honey.

Throughout their lives, the Mbuti are always aware of the profound importance of the forest. A father celebrates the birth of a new baby by bringing it gifts of home-made bark-cloth and bathes it in the juice of forest vines. When girls celebrate their 'entry to womanhood' they chant a line of song to the forest and then wait for the trees to reply with an echo. When a young man first becomes a successful hunter, his forehead is cut and rubbed with a paste of forest herbs and ash, symbolising the forest's presence in the human body. People take care not to 'insult' the forest by behaving badly, making too much noise, or destroying any plants without good reason. If something bad happens – for example, illness, death or poor hunting – the whole group holds a special ceremony in which they 'sing to the forest' to make the relationship harmonious again.

Although the Mbuti Pygmies have a self-contained culture, for hundreds of years they have had a lot of contact with the Bantu people who are farmers and craftspeople living in permanent villages in clearings in the rain forest. The Mbuti provide the villagers with meat, honey and other forest goods; in return the villagers give the Mbuti pottery, metal pans, knives and arrowheads. They also often do occasional jobs for the villagers; and the villagers help the Mbuti if they need to have any dealings with government authorities. The villagers tend to regard the forest with great distaste and fear.

Since the 1950s many new settlers have moved into the fringes of central Africa's rain forest. Mostly they are farmers who grow 'cash crops' which are sold abroad. These newcomers bring a new outlook, which could spoil the traditional relationship between the Mbuti and the original Bantu villagers.

The first European logging companies are now arriving there. They are expected to destroy great stretches of forest; and their presence will also encourage large numbers of other outsiders to move into the area, bringing both new diseases and pressures to change to a more 'modern' lifestyle.

Some Pygmy men have been keen to work in the first sawmills that have opened. Others are being forced to help build the new roads which are needed by the loggers. As a result, these people must settle in the shanty-villages which are built nearby, abandoning their usual way of life. There are also reports of government projects to force the Pygmies to give up their nomadic existence, to wear 'civilised' clothes and to become what they define as 'normal'. Another problem is the creation of National Parks to protect the rain forests: in most cases they result in the removal of all human inhabitants, including the Pygmies.

Some observers suggest that Pygmy culture is robust enough to survive many outside threats and pressures. However, it is totally bound up with the forest which they love, and which supplies everything they need; so if – or, more accurately, when – the rain forest of central Africa is destroyed, inevitably the Pygmy way of life will also have to die.

Fire and the Forest Lord

Mbuti Pygmy, Zaire

We call him Tore, but he has many other names: Arebati, Baatsi, Grandfather – what does it matter? He is Lord of the Forest, its heart, its spirit, its protector, our protector. He is always there, and without him surely the whole Forest and everything in it would die.

Now, back in the Age of Beginning, it was Lord Tore who created Fire. He was really proud! He spent many hours, many days, watching new dreams dancing in its golden flames.

Because of Fire, he neglected the Forest. But in the end he heard the trees calling him back. They called quietly yet urgently, sad with longing for their master.

So Tore made himself a swing of vines, creepers and lianas. It was the most amazing swing in the whole world: it carried him high, high, right up to the tops of the trees: so high that Tore could see the entire Forest spread out below like a throbbing, rustling sea; so high that he was almost touching the sun!

Up and down, up and down he swung, singing love songs to his trees and creatures. Now a great happiness washed down through them all. And for a while, Lord Tore forgot about Fire . . .

While he was away, he had left Fire burning in the care of Old Mother. This one, she understood how much it mattered to Tore, her son. She did her best to look after it.

But she was a very old woman. Watching the mysterious flames was too much for her. Her head began to nod: soon she was day-dreaming; next she was fast asleep.

And while Old Mother slept, a man came along, an ordinary man of the Forest. He could scarcely believe his eyes when he saw Fire. What a marvel! He must try to get it, he must have it for his people!

Soft as a leopard, this man crept past Old Mother. He snatched Fire up in his bare hands; he laughed with excitement, he raced away.

In the emptiness, in the darkness, Old Mother felt cold: she
woke up. 'Tore, Tore!' she screamed.

The Forest Lord came rushing down on his swing. As soon as
he saw what had happened, he hurtled through the air after the
man. He caught him – he snatched Fire back! . . . Ah, but his
heart was too kind: he let the thief go free.

This man, the thief, he raced straight back to his camp and told
everyone his story. As soon as it was finished, his brother stood
up. 'Tell me the way to Lord Tore's camp,' said he. 'Tomorrow *I*
will go straight there. By nightfall, I swear I will bring this
amazing Fire back to you.'

So at dawn he set off along the secret trails that led to Tore's
camp. He saw Fire; he saw Old Mother dozing. Softly, softly, he
stole the fire and ran away. Then just as before, Old Mother felt
cold, woke up and shrieked for Tore; and the Forest Lord came
swinging down, snatched Fire back but let the thief go free.

The brother went home, and again the tale was told. When it
was over, a third man stood up.

This last man's name was Doru. He was not like other people.
It was said he could do strange, impossible things; for he himself
was filled with mysterious Forest-power.

'*I* will bring you Fire,' said Doru.

He went to a storage pot and took from it many black feathers,
feathers of a raven. He stuck them carefully over his chest and
over his arms. Then he stood very still, letting the magic raven-
force mingle with his own. When this was done, he leaped into
the air – and began to fly!

He flew as high as the heavens and as far as the horizon. Soon
he came to Tore's camp, where Old Mother was sleeping.

At first, everything was as before. Doru stole Fire; he ran away.
Old Mother felt cold; she woke and screeched for Tore to catch the
thief. Tore came sweeping down after Doru, wild and angry on
his liana-swing. But from that moment, everything was different.

Doru in his raven feathers flew up to the mountains: Tore hurtled after, but failed to catch him. Then Doru soared up to the very sky and down, down to the abyss below. Still Tore failed to catch him, still he failed to retrieve his Fire.

Then Lord Tore was exhausted. He collapsed into the branches of a tree. He admitted he was beaten.

So Doru threw off his feathers and went home. Everyone was astonished and thrilled to see the Fire he carried. He split it and shared it out, a portion to every family. Since then it has always been passed down, father to son, mother to daughter, age by age.

But our Lord Tore was left only sorrow and anger. He could not believe that his own people could cheat him with such tricks. And when he got home, even greater anguish awaited him: Old Mother was dead. She had died of cold, all because Fire was stolen.

From that day on, people also began to die, one after another. They died because Lord Tore wished it, in revenge for Old Mother's death.

So Fire and Death have lived side by side among people ever since.

The Most Beautiful
Song in the Forest

Mbuti Pygmy, Zaire

Hush: listen. Can you hear the Forest?

Leaves dropping, softly, softly; rain pattering on the leaves. Creatures scuttling, creeping; the cracking of twigs; monkeys chattering, bees humming. Lianas creak as they sway in the wind, and far, far off an elephant calls.

Listen to them all, my friend. Ah, but there is one sound you can never, ever hear, because it has been destroyed for ever – it is extinct. And that is the Most Beautiful Song in the Forest.

Not so long ago, this song still lived and a young boy heard it. It was so unbelievably sweet, so exquisite . . . Ach! How can mere words describe it? It made the boy want to cry with grief and dance about with joy, all at the same time. It was full of everything: love, longing and despair; the scent of damp earth, mother's milk, flowers . . . I tell you, everything, *everything* was contained in that song.

And as soon as the boy heard it, he had but one desire: he must find the singer.

So the boy walked through the soft green lights of the Forest, following the sweetness of the song. Ahead, it always seemed to be just ahead of him. But at last it came to rest in a clearing. There on the ground stood the singer: a small, plain brown bird.

The boy whispered to the bird, 'How wonderfully you sing!'

The bird was silent now. But it fixed the boy with its bright eye.

Then the boy whispered to it again, this time making gentle, clucking little love noises like a mother to her baby. He reached into his belt and held out a handful of seeds. The bird flew down and took the food: the boy offered more. And so they went on, over and over like this for some time, until at last the boy and the bird were friends.

'I wish you would come home with me,' said the boy. He spoke from his heart, and the little bird understood. With a soft fluttering of its brown wings, it perched on top of his head. And there it stayed, as the boy walked happily, through the Forest, back to his family's camp.

His father was waiting for him there. He was angry. 'Where ever have you been?' he scolded. 'Your mother thought you were lost.' And then: 'What ever is that stupid thing stuck on top of your head?'

The boy only answered, 'Listen!'

Almost at once, the little bird began to sing. Sweet as spring water; deep as the oldest mysteries; strong, sweetly strong as the sap of a thousand-thousand ancient trees. For a few moments, the boy's father lost his irritation: tears even came to his eyes. But as soon as the bird stopped its song, his face clouded again.

'Yes, very nice I'm sure,' he grumbled. 'But I'm supposed to prepare myself for a hunting expedition tomorrow. The other men are all ready; only *I* have had to miss the preparations, all because your mother was sick with worry about you getting lost!'

His voice rose: the last words came out with a bitter shout; and then he stamped off. The little bird stared after him for a moment, measuring his anger. Then, to the boy's dismay, it spread its wings and flew away.

However, the next day the boy heard its wonderful song again. The sound of it made his heart soar. Once again he spent long hours searching for it through the trees. Again, when he found it, he quickly coaxed it back to friendship with morsels of food. And again, of its free will, the bird went with him back to the camp.

This time, his father was in a good mood. He was with the other men, celebrating the killing of two large antelopes, taking his share of cutting up the rich meat. The boy brought the bird to him and urged him to listen to it singing. He didn't shout this time, but only turned away with a scornful laugh.

'Let me get on with my work,' he said shortly. 'You should be watching and learning with me, my son, learning to be a man. Take that baby's pet away!'

As on the previous day, the bird seemed startled by the sharpness of his words. Almost at once, it flew away.

The next day was the same. The boy spent the best part of his time looking for the bird which sang the Most Beautiful Song in the Forest, befriending it, and bringing it home to share with his family. And just as before, his father was too irritable to hear the sweetness of its singing and frightened the creature away.

Nevertheless, by the fourth day, the boy and the bird had built up a deep friendship. They had learned to trust and understand each other. 'Ignore my father,' the boy told it. 'This time, please don't be bothered by his nasty words. This time, please stay a little longer, so that my mother and all my other relations may enjoy the magic of your singing.'

The little bird cocked its head and stared at him as if to say, 'I will.' But as soon as they got back to the camp, they found the boy's father waiting for them, with thunder in his eyes.

'There you are, just as I thought!' he snapped. 'Off with that stupid bird again, always wasting your time!'

And with that, he snatched the bird from his son's head and hurled it with all his force to the ground. He killed it!

The boy gave a shriek of anguish; but that was not the end of his sorrow. For the next moment his father gave a dreadful cry of pain – and he himself dropped dead!

Ah my friend, in this sad tale you will hear a lesson.

The man killed the bird; and with it he killed its song, the Most Beautiful Song in the Forest. In killing the song, he wounded the Forest most dreadfully – and the Forest took its revenge.

So don't hurt the Forest, don't destroy it, for its pain will always come back to you.

The Company of Chimpanzees

 ## The Naked Ape
Ngbandi, Zaire/Congo

There was a scientist visiting us the other week, talking about chimpanzees. She told us they've found that body for body, brain for brain, there's scarcely any difference between chimps and humans. And you know, she expected us to be impressed and amazed!

But what she told us was nothing new. Here, on the edge of the forest, chimpanzees are no strangers to us. We know things about them that even your scientists certainly don't. Like, back in the old days, chimpanzees and people, we were all one species.

And yet . . . even then, not everyone was quite the same. I'll tell you what the only difference was: there were some who liked wearing clothes, and others who preferred to go naked.

Well, there was this man who was the sort who preferred to have nothing on. Clothes made him feel unnatural, uncomfortable. He couldn't care less what other people thought of him: he just wanted to be himself.

After a while, the man got married, and it so happened that the wife and her family were of the clothes-wearing kind. The wife respected her husband for what he was, and he respected her. But it was a different matter with her family, the man's in-laws. They laughed at naked people, said they were vulgar and uncivilised; and the man knew it.

So whenever he went to stay with his wife's folk, he always took care to arrive after dark. That way, they couldn't see that he had nothing on. And to make sure they didn't catch him out, he used to take a boy with him. This boy's job was to wake the man up before dawn, so that he could leave for home before his in-laws had a chance to see his nakedness in the morning light. He paid the boy well in the middle of the night by giving him a generous portion of the delicious food which his mother-in-law always cooked.

But on one visit his wife's mother cooked a fresh chicken in the most extravagantly delicious way: he had never tasted anything like it before. He couldn't resist it, he couldn't help it: he gobbled the whole lot up himself.

The boy hung about through the night, hungry, waiting for his share. It didn't come. So he peeped into the hut and saw his master snoring away contentedly, belching softly, with a full belly. Then he knew he had been cheated.

Spitting a few silent curses at the man through the darkness, he crept away.

Without the boy to rouse him, the man did not wake up until it was completely light. In a panic he leaped up from his bed. But he was too late: his in-laws were already all gathered around him, staring, pointing at his nakedness, laughing until their sides split.

My goodness, he was embarrassed! He rushed out, not even taking time to say goodbye to his wife. He went away, far away; he went to live in the depths of the forest.

He was the first chimpanzee.

 ## Sister Chimpanzee
Daobli Village, Ivory Coast

Long, long ago, when my great-great-grandfather was still young, the oldest daughter of the village chief went for a walk in the forest – and never came back.

They sent out search parties, but no one could find her. Her mother wept and called, she beat her breast in grief; but nothing could bring the lost girl home. In the end, the chief accepted that his beloved daughter must be dead.

The whole village went into mourning. But before all the ceremonies were done, a great commotion started up in the forest: shrieks, cries and hoots. The chief had always clutched at the last straws of hope, and he believed in signs and omens. He listened to the uproar for a while. Then, calling his people to follow, he led the way into the forest.

Through the trees they went. The sounds grew ever stronger. Then all at once they came to a clearing – and found themselves staring at a troupe of chimpanzees.

There were huge ones, old ones, stooped and shaggy. There were young ones, big eared, neat headed. Light filtered through the trees: in it, their black fur shone. Suddenly, the crowd of them scattered – and there in their midst, smiling, stood the lost girl!

What wonder had happened?

For she was still the same one, the pride of the chief's heart . . . yet she had changed – oh, how she had changed!

She had discarded her fine clothes and ornaments. Her lovely face was just the same, but below the waist, her body had shrunk, shrivelled and distorted, and grown a thick coating of fur. She had half turned into a chimpanzee!

'Father,' she called in her own sweet voice, 'listen. Come to me: I want to say goodbye, and I want to introduce my new family. When I was lost in the forest, these creatures rescued me. They treated me with the greatest kindness, they fed me with delicious food, they protected me, they healed my wounds, they taught me their language. I like their simple ways, their wildness, the honesty of their lives: I like it far better than my old life in the village with all its rituals and pomp. I want to stay with my new relations, for they have opened their hearts and welcomed me as their sister.'

At these strange words, the chief and his wife both wept, and all the villagers wept too. Yet when he saw how his beloved daughter's eyes shone with happiness, the chief knew he could not refuse her wish.

'Then stay with them, my girl,' he replied at last, 'and may your happiness stay with you always. Tell your new family that they have become our kin too. From this time on, for all time, I swear that no one in our village shall ever hurt them.'

And so it was. The chief's daughter lived with the chimpanzees for the rest of her life.

Yes, all this happened long ago. Much of the great rain forest in our country has been cut down since then. But here, just beyond the edge of the village where Sister Chimpanzee once lived, you can see a great stretch of it is still standing. The government protects the trees, but it is we who protect the chimps. Over there we keep a small shrine to them. And there is not a person in Daobli who would let them come to harm, for to us they will always be family.

The Chimpanzee Ancestor
Makere, Zaire

There was once a man who was out hunting elephants when he got lost in the forest. He went this way, he went that way; he walked for days and days; still he couldn't find his way home.

By now he was exhausted and desperate. His feet were sore and he longed for a proper meal of cooked meat instead of the wild fruits and roots which were all he could find in the forest.

He decided to climb a tree. From the top, maybe he would be able to see smoke rising in the distance, which would be the sign of a village.

He cut himself a sling of lianas and began to clamber up the huge, bare trunk. Slowly, slowly, he shinned up it until at last he reached the lowest branch. He reached out and grabbed it . . .

But at that moment the liana sling broke. Now there was nothing to support him but his own hands. He swung from the branch, swaying heavily, helplessly in the evening wind. He felt his fingers would surely break, or his arms would be wrenched out of their sockets. Yet if he let go, he would drop like a stone to the ground: he would certainly die.

'Help!' he screamed, though there was no chance of anyone hearing him. Yet even a man who knows he must die still clings to the last shred of hope. 'Help!' he called again.

The very next moment he was astonished to hear someone! They were hurrying closer . . . then his own tree shook. He tried to turn his head, but it was impossible. There was a noise just above him. He looked up – and found himself staring into the eyes of a male chimpanzee!

The chimp stretched down a long arm. It grasped the man's wrist in its own strong fingers. Then it pulled, it heaved. Suddenly he was safe, clasped to a huge, furry chest, resting against the branch of the tree.

The man was not afraid. The chimpanzee held him tightly and carried him down to the base of the tree. There, carefully, it laid him down and collected a pile of leaves to put under his head as a pillow. Then it was gone – but a short time later it came back carrying a bunch of luscious fruit. Gently it lifted the man until he was sitting, prised open his lips and squeezed the juices from the fruit into his mouth.

For several days they stayed together like this, the man and the chimp. At last the man recovered a little, but he was still too weak to walk. The chimpanzee lifted him onto its shoulders and carried him through the trees until they came to the nearest village.

Now, this village was not of his own people: it belonged to an enemy tribe. When they recognised him for what he was, surely they would kill him! But he was wrong.

For these people believed that chimpanzees were really the spirits of their dead ancestors, re-born into a new shape. When they saw one carrying an unknown man into their midst, they welcomed him as a gift from heaven.

They took him in and the chief put the man into the care of his only daughter. She nursed him carefully until he was fully restored to health.

When he was better, the man began to hunt elephants again. If he had been a good hunter before, now he was brilliant. It was as if the chimpanzee had given him extra power: each time he set out, he found an elephant trail easily, and each one he followed resulted in a kill. The chief and his people were delighted. Each elephant meant enough meat to feed the whole village for weeks.

The chief honoured the man by letting him marry his daughter. They had many children. The village grew prosperous and happy, for the chimpanzee-ancestors continued to bless them with good luck.

The Making of the Palm Trees
Ngbandi, Zaire/Congo

Nzapa is our Father. He was there in the beginning. He made the world, the plants, the animals, the people, the spirits. He gave us our laws; he taught us how to live; he decides our fates, the fates of everyone.

Listen: there is Sky, there is Earth, there is Clear Water, there is Dark Water, there is Fortune, there is Peace. Pray to all these gods every morning, my children; but above all, remember your prayers to Nzapa. For he is the High God, he is the Father of everything.

Once Nzapa made for himself four sons, and each of these sons had the shape of a magnificent palm tree.

Time passed: the great Father felt hungry, very hungry. He had no wife of his own, but by now each of his sons was married. So he called to his daughters-in-law to cook him some food.

The four women obeyed; and when the food was ready, each one asked her husband to take it to Nzapa.

The first son's name was Ndimba. When he saw the meal his wife had cooked, his mouth watered. He ate the largest portion himself and took only the left-overs to his father.

The second son's name was Ngara. When his own wife's meal was ready he behaved in exactly the same selfish way as his brother. He ate as much of it as he had room for, and took only scraps to Nzapa.

Pe, the third son, was just as bad. While his wife was cooking, his stomach rumbled: he gobbled up the best of the food for himself, and took only the leanest pickings to his father.

But the last son, Kpmon, was honest and dutiful. As soon as his wife had finished her work, he took the whole dish, steaming hot, straight to Nzapa. He himself did not touch a single morsel.

The old Father ate. He noticed everything. More time passed. Then he called his sons together.

'My children,' he said, 'I created you all the same; yet as the years have passed, each of you has grown different. Now there will be not one palm tree on the banks of the Oubangui River, but four kinds. Listen which will belong to each of you.

'Pe, you will be the wine-palm. Men will cut holes in your body and drain out your sap to make wine. If this hurts you, my son, remember how you have hurt me by your greed.

'Ngara, you will be the liana. Women will cut you and plait you; they will twist you into baskets. If this makes you feel uncomfortable, my son, remember the discomfort I felt when I saw how you had cheated me.

'Ndimba, you will be the raffia-palm. People will weave you into beds and lie on you. If this is painful, remember my pain when you gave me only scraps of food to eat.

'But Kpmon, you have been everything a son should be. You have looked after me and given me all the best of your food. Because of this, you will be the oil-palm. You will grow old and strong. Each year, people will pick your nuts, but they will not hurt you. And though the nuts themselves will wilt and die year by year, the oil that is squeezed from them will stay fresh and delicious for ever.'

Thus Nzapa our Father spoke; and so it was.

What a Terrible Life in the Forest!

Mbuti Pygmy, Zaire

Have you been outside this part of the Forest yet, to the villages? Have you met any of the people who live there?

Of course, you'll want to judge them for yourself. Most of them are okay – apart from one big fault: they're so high and mighty, they reckon they're the greatest folk on Earth, and they look down their noses at us Forest people as if we were scum. But listen . . . *they're* the ones who are really the idiots!

Mind you, they're quite clever at making all sorts of useful things. So when we need new tools, we usually go and see them: we pay for what we want with bush-meat and honey. They can't wait to get their hands on it – in fact, without us, they'd have no meat or honey at all. You'll never guess why: they won't go hunting for themselves, because they're too *scared* of the Forest!

They reckon it's full of evil spirits. Have you ever heard anything so ridiculous? There's nothing evil *here*! The Forest is our father, our mother, our friend . . .

Anyway, these snooty, stupid villagers – we love to play tricks on them. We get everything we want from them – and we have a really good laugh behind their backs . . .

There was this old fellow called Cephu, and one day he fancied some rice to eat for a change, so he thought he'd nip across to the nearest village and get some.

There's always plenty of rice to be had out there: they grow it in their fields. But of course, the villagers aren't that stupid: they don't give it away for nothing. A sack of rice costs a big hunk of bush-meat. Everybody knows that.

But Cephu, he was getting lazy in his old age. He couldn't be bothered to go out and catch an antelope to pay for it – not even a little monkey. So, the cheeky old devil, he set off empty-handed.

He walked for a few hours, and at last came to the village. There he met a big man he knew well: his name was Lukamba.

'Hello there, Cephu,' said he. 'What have you got for me today?'

'I'm afraid I haven't got a thing,' replied Cephu.

'What, no gifts for me!'

Cephu looked very gloomy. 'Ah, Lukamba, sometimes it isn't easy for us Mbuti to bring what we ought to, not even for our most respected friends. You know what a terrible life we have in the Forest!'

'Yes, yes,' agreed Lukamba. 'I know. Which ever way you look, there is nothing but trees and more trees. Then there is the silence; the constant rain storms and everything always so damp and dripping; the lack of sunlight . . .'

'But there are far worse things than that,' prompted Cephu.

'No, no, don't mention them!'

'You know what I mean,' Cephu went on, ignoring the other's agitation. 'Spirits: *evil* spirits! The forest is full of them, Lukamba.'

'I pity you all, Cephu my friend! I pity your people for your dark and dangerous lives.'

'When you hear what happened to me on my way here today, Lukamba, you will pity me even more!

'Listen, when I set out, I had a whole antelope loaded on my back. I planned to give it to you. My brothers and I killed it yesterday and I said to them, "It is high time I took a gift of the best quality meat to our noble friend Lukamba. Think of all he does for us. When one of us needs to earn some money to buy something from the outside world, he is kind enough to let us work in his fields. When we need new cooking pots or hunting knives, he is always more than happy to bargain over a price for such things. Maybe he will have a little rice to spare in return for such a gift as this, or maybe he won't. What does it matter either way? Such good meat should be put aside and taken to him, without question."'

'How kind of you to think of me, Cephu, how very kind!' exclaimed Lukamba. 'So tell me, what happened to this fine animal you were bringing; what happened to *you* on the way?'

'Ah, Lukamba, I had walked for scarcely an hour from my camp, but already I was in a very lonely place of dark, towering tree trunks and shivering vines. The silence was crowding in on me. From the corner of my eye, I saw shadows darting in and out behind the furthest trees. And then, suddenly, it came upon me! An evil spirit!'

Lukamba gave a shudder but he said nothing. Cephu went on:

'"Give me your meat!" shrieked this foul apparition. "Give me everything you have!" "No," I said, as boldly as I dared, "this meat happens to be for a very dear friend of mine who lives in the village. I will defend it for him with my life!"

'Maybe a lesser man would have run away – but I faced the spirit head on, seized my knife, and challenged it to a fight.'

'Good for you, Cephu. Did you succeed in killing it?'

'Ah, Lukamba, you know that Forest spirits are far wickeder, far more powerful than anything that exists outside! No, no, it is absolutely impossible to kill one. However, after a long and terrible fight, I did at last succeed in driving it away . . .'

'Well done!'

'. . . Ah, but it was only for a few moments. Before I had walked on much further, it appeared again. And this time it was in a new shape. It is hard for me to tell you this: it had assumed the form of my own dear, poor, long-dead grandmother!'

'What an outrage!'

'Yes indeed, Lukamba; but you have not heard everything yet. "Cephu, my boy," my grandmother said (and even her voice was right, Lukamba; the spirit was very convincing), "I see you have just what I need, a nice joint of meat. Hand it over to me quickly, lad, for I am very hungry." "I can't," I said, "it's for my good friend Lukamba who lives in the village." "Tut-tut," she said, "your old grandma is much more important than any friend you choose to hang around with, even if he is a villager. Give the meat here to me at once!" And with that, she wrenched the whole basket right off my back!

'What could I do? She looked so convincing, this apparition, so like my grandma. Lukamba, I ask you, what would *you* have done? Would you lower yourself to arguing with an aged woman? Would you dare to fight with an ancestor? Would you deny food to one who was the spitting image of your own mother's mother – the one who had rocked you and sung you to sleep, night after night, when you were a tiny babe in arms?'

'My dear Cephu: it is unthinkable!'

'Lukamba, I knew you would understand and sympathise: you are a noble and compassionate man. So you see, I had no choice but to let her go, taking away all the delicious meat that was really meant for you.

'And then, to add insult to injury, she was still in sight of me, when she turned back into her true evil spirit shape! I raced after it, I fought it again . . . But the Forest spirits are so unbelievably strong . . . Lukamba, I have to confess that after several hours I had no choice but to give up. I was forced to tell the spirit to keep the meat, if it would only spare my life.'

'You were right, Cephu, of course you were right.'

'So that is why, on this visit, I am so sorry that I have nothing to offer you after all. But I still wanted to come and pay my respects to you.'

'Well!' exclaimed Lukamba. 'After all you have endured in your efforts to bring me some meat, I insist, Cephu, that you must at least carry a sack of rice home with you. And I see your hunting knife is also missing from your belt, my friend?'

'Oh, don't ask me about that! I am ashamed to say that the evil spirit even stole that from me as well.'

'Then you shall let me give you a new one. A sack of the best rice and a fine new knife: I shall send my boy to fetch these things for you straight away.'

'Lukamba, you are too kind!'

'Nonsense, my dear fellow: not after all the terrors you have been through! Of course, ahem, you know I myself would go and kill my own meat in the Forest if I could; but they say that these evil spirits are even more deadly to us villagers!'

So Cephu, the old rascal, went home a happy man. He carried all that he'd come for and even more – and he hadn't had to pay a single thing in return.

But Lukamba the villager, he was happy too. The tale he had heard sent genuine shivers down his spine: he was really glad that he'd lived all his life amongst the neat fields and plantations, safely beyond the edge of the dark trees.

Oh, what a terrible, terrible life those poor Mbuti must live in the Forest!

The Forest Peoples
of South-East Asia

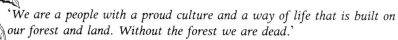

'We are a people with a proud culture and a way of life that is built on our forest and land. Without the forest we are dead.'

Dayak tribal elder

Once much of South-East Asia was almost completely covered in rain forest; but vast stretches have been destroyed in Burma, Cambodia, Laos, the Philippines, Thailand and Vietnam. Nevertheless, until recently in three countries much of the original forest has remained untouched: these are Malaysia, Indonesia and Papua New Guinea.

The biggest expanse is on New Guinea – the second largest island in the world. The eastern half forms most of the independent country of Papua New Guinea; while the western part, known as Irian Jaya, has belonged to Indonesia since 1963. About three-quarters of the island's forest is still undisturbed. Its rich wildlife includes tree kangaroos, flying foxes, crocodiles, possums, spectacular birds of paradise and the world's largest butterfly.

About 4 million people live on New Guinea, divided amongst numerous different tribes. Many of these have until very recently lived in almost total isolation from all outsiders. As many as a thousand different languages are spoken on the island.

Most of the people live by farming. Their crops include coconuts, yams, taro, sago and bananas, and they also keep pigs. They catch fish and hunt wild pigs, wallabies and many types of birds.

The people traditionally organise their lives around their family and their village. Most tribes have no formal leaders: problems are discussed and decisions made by all the men in the group. Warfare between different tribes is common. In some cases the fighting may be ritualistic and fairly harmless; but where there is a serious grievance battles can be very fierce. Some groups regard eating the flesh of their slain enemies as the supreme act of vengeance for a wrong-doing; others – known as 'head-hunters' – preserve the heads of any enemies they have killed, as a symbol of their victories.

Traditional religion generally centres on belief in the super-natural, including ghosts of the ancestors and spirits of rocks, trees and other natural features. Many of these spirits are regarded as evil and dangerous and can only be overcome by magic.

The Danis live in a very remote valley deep in the forested highlands of western New Guinea (Irian Jaya). They build round wooden houses with thatched roofs. They have no use for metal, but make highly sophisticated tools of stone, wood and bone, enabling them to be very skilled at farming and forestry. Their carefully irrigated fields produce cabbages, sweet potatoes, carrots and taro, but their most important activity is pig keeping. The men reckon their wealth in pigs, and when a woman marries, pigs are exchanged in payment between the bridal families. These animals are treated with the greatest affection, like family pets.

Dani society is friendly and closely knit, and takes good care of all its dependants. Polygamy (the practice of one man marrying several wives) is common, but women and men live separately. At night the men all sleep together in the loft above their exclusive meeting house. The men wear virtually no clothes; the women wear string skirts and, for religious reasons, are careful to keep their backs covered with long, draped string nets woven from tree-bark and decorated with coloured orchid roots.

Some years ago, missionaries succeeded in persuading many Danis to convert to Christianity. However, following the destruction of villages and farms in order to build forest airstrips for the missionaries' planes, the relationship turned sour, and there were killings on both sides. Today about 100,000 Danis have rejected the outside world and successfully revived their own way of life, although some still practise their own unique brand of Christianity.

The island of Borneo, which is only slightly smaller than New Guinea, is split between three countries: Malaysia, Indonesia and the tiny state of Brunei. Its wildlife includes orang-utans, gibbons, mouse-deer, elephants and rhinos. Like New Guinea, it is inhabited by a great variety of different peoples.

The Ibans and the Dayaks are two of the largest groups. Their main activity is rice farming, and they also keep pigs and chickens and catch fish.

Both groups organise their village life around the longhouse. This is a huge building, perhaps 100 metres long, and raised on tall stilts about five metres above the ground. Within the longhouse, many different families each have their own private apartment. Outside there is a long verandah on which different households meet to chat and work side by side at tasks such as pounding rice, making nets or weaving baskets. Each village contains two or more longhouses.

Dayak and Iban societies are fairly free and relaxed, and treat all their members more or less equally. Traditional dress for both women and men is a *sarong* (skirt). Although men play a more important role in decision making, the women's opinions are taken into account. Each village is led by a headman, chosen by his fellows, and working with the agreement of anyone who is interested enough to take part in village meetings.

Their religion is based on a belief in spirits – particularly the spirit of rice – and also spirits of the ancestors, of living people, and of the natural world.

At one time carefully organised warfare and head-hunting was fairly common among both peoples.

The governments of Malaysia and Indonesia state that their official policies are to preserve much of their natural rain forests; however, both predict that very significant proportions will be destroyed to make room for their growing populations, and because of the need for economic development.

Conservationists and economic experts warn that cutting trees for timber in all parts of Malaysia will have destroyed most of its natural forests by the year 2000. There are still about 220,000 tribal people living in the Malaysian part of Borneo. Official government policy is to put pressure on them 'to lead more settled and progressive lives'. Some are indeed happy to enter modern society with its benefits such as education and medicine. However, recently many Dayaks, Ibans, nomadic Penans and other tribes have organised major protests to try to stop the loggers from devastating their forest homelands. Hundreds of these tribal people have been arrested and sent to prison.

In Irian Jaya (Indonesian New Guinea) both the rain forests and the tribal peoples are in danger of disappearing because of the government's plan to cut and sell as much timber as possible; other areas are being destroyed by mining. Another major problem is the government's policy of 'transmigration', in which vast numbers of outsiders from Indonesia's most overcrowded islands are being moved to Irian Jaya, where they are expected to turn the forest into farms and to work for logging companies. Local tribespeople are being forced off their own land and pressurised to join the newcomers' way of life.

In Papua New Guinea, most of the land is actually owned by local tribespeople. With the support and help of overseas campaigners, these people are now beginning to refuse permission to the numerous logging companies who wish to cut down their forests.

The Forest is His

Iban, *Malaysian Borneo*

How dare they come here and cut the trees down? It is outrageous! Oh, I know they say they have the government's permission . . . but the forest does not belong to the government!

No, no, I'm not saying that it belongs to us either – it belongs to Pulang Gana. This is the sacred truth. Our ancestors have passed it down to us. Let me tell you how they discovered it.

In ancient times there lived seven brothers. In those days, the forest in this country went on and on for ever, without any end.

These brothers, they wanted to cut some of it down to make themselves a farm. So they chose a small patch of land, took up their axes and began to hew the trees.

Night came and the brothers went home to sleep. The next morning they walked back to their clearing – but it had disappeared! Overnight, the trees had all grown back. The creepers and vines, the lianas, the shrubs, the ferns, all the undergrowth: everything grew thicker and greener than ever before!

The brothers were puzzled, but they did not give up. They set to work again: cutting, chopping, hacking through the forest. Again at the day's end they went home – and returned the next morning to find that the forest had restored itself overnight.

All this happened three times. On the fourth night, the seven men stayed on the edge of the clearing, hiding and watching.

Very soon they saw a spirit.

The spirit moved among the fallen trunks, the stripped bark, the wood chippings. He touched them all. Under the power of his touch, all things sprang back to life.

At first the seven brothers were very angry. You understand how it was: they badly wanted this farm to grow rice. They were prepared to do anything for it. They leaped from their hiding place. They were not afraid to fight the spirit!

But he stopped them by the simple power of his words:

'Stay! I am Pulang Gana. Hear me! Every tree, every thing that grows is mine. Beyond the forest, to the furthest horizon, south, north, east and west, the whole Earth belongs to me. No living being may ever use any part of my realm without my permission.'

Then he told them his law: people who have need of his things must bring him gifts and offerings. If such things please him, maybe he will lend them some land . . .

Lend it, you notice: not give it.

Pah! These men from the timber companies who come here, stealing wood, stealing land . . .

We ask ourselves, how do they stand with Pulang Gana? Will he not take his revenge on them in the end?

The Superman of Sarawak

Dayak, Malaysian Borneo

There was a lady called Gumiloh. She was proud, she was beautiful, and she was clever. Lots of young men courted her: one even persuaded her to make half a promise of marriage. Yet, in her heart, she felt that none was really her match.

One day she was working on the longhouse verandah, laying out piles of freshly cut rice in the sun, when she felt a stranger's eyes upon her. Looking up, she saw an arrogant looking youth.

'Who are you?' she called to him.

'I am Kichapi,' he replied.

'Well then, Kichapi: what do you want of me?'

'I have fallen in love with you, lady. I want to marry you.'

Gumiloh laughed. 'Oh, if that's your game, I'm afraid you're too late – for I'm already betrothed to Bilantur.'

'Then un-betroth yourself, lady. Whoever he is, I'm a much better man than him.'

'Oh yes?' said Gumiloh. 'Do you expect me to believe that? I don't know even the first thing about you!'

'No,' said Kichapi, 'but I'm certain you'll be impressed when you hear the amazing story of my life.'

'It takes more than you might think to impress Gumiloh,' she retorted. Nonetheless she left her rice and came over to sit on the edge of the high verandah. 'But do go ahead.'

'Well firstly,' said Kichapi, 'there is the matter of my birth. I was seven whole years growing inside my mother – and when I was born, I was already fully grown into the handsome fellow you see before you.'

Gumiloh let out a guffaw. 'You don't expect me to believe that!'

'Why not, lady? But let me continue. The minute I first saw the light of day, I jumped straight up and ran off into the forest.'

'Into the forest! What, all alone? Didn't any wild creature eat you? Didn't you get lost?'

'Not at all,' said Kichapi. 'I was quite safe. I'm not afraid of the forest. But *you* would be afraid, Gumiloh my only love, if you'd met the fierce creatures that I fell in with.'

'So what were they? Wait, let me guess: tigers? crocodiles?'

'No, none of those. I'm talking about *giants*.'

'No! Are there really such things as giants?'

'Oh there are, Gumiloh, I promise you. They live deep, deep in the forest. You wouldn't know, for you have never been there. These two that I befriended – a he-giant and a she-giant – they each had seven heads.'

'Be off with you, Kichapi! Honestly, I've never heard such stories! Why didn't the monsters eat you up then?'

'Well, actually they did. Each of them took a turn at swallowing me – but I just slipped straight through their bodies and jumped out the other end! After that, they took a liking to me. They begged me to go and live with them, which I did, and then they adopted me as their grandson. In fact, that's where my home is now, in their cave, a hundred days' journey away.'

'Oh yes: so how did you manage to get here then?'

'Well, my love, I was fated to meet you: I came by magic. You see, in front of the giants' cave stands a tall palm tree. The giants made me promise never to climb it. Ah, you know how it is when something is forbidden, Gumiloh: it makes the temptation impossible to resist . . . Today the giants both left me to go out hunting. I could not bear it any longer, not knowing what was the tree's great secret. So I leaped onto its trunk and shinned my way up. As I climbed, the tree began to grow: higher and higher. It seemed I would never reach its top. But at long, long last the end came in sight: it bent right over until it touched the ground. I jumped off and found myself right here, at your house, Gumiloh. You can't send me away now!'

'I most certainly can!' exclaimed Gumiloh, jumping up. 'I've never heard such nonsense and lies! Just be off with you, Kichapi – and don't you dare come chasing me again with your tales!'

A few months passed. Gumiloh went down the winding river to her forest garden with two of her uncles. They planned to cut some sugar-cane to take home.

But as soon as they arrived at the garden, she saw a magnificent orang-utan sitting in a tree. She was enchanted by the animal's shaggy, red-brown fur and the intelligent light that shone from its eyes. With gentle words and gestures, she tried to coax it down. The creature came to her willingly, and took fruit from her hand.

Before the afternoon was over, she had persuaded her uncles to let her take the wild thing home with her in their boat.

Everyone in the village crowded round to see her marvellous new pet. Gumiloh made a tremendous fuss of it: she let it eat rice and vegetables from her own plate; and at night she even persuaded her many admirers to let it have the best loft in the bachelors' sleeping-house. The orang-utan took to following her around everywhere, and if ever anyone raised a voice or a hand to her, it always leaped to her defence. In fact, it was so protective that on her next trip down-stream to her garden, she took only the orang-utan to guard her from the many dangers of the forest.

But when they got there and she set to work, cutting the ripe canes, what a surprise she had! She turned round to find that the orang-utan had shed the whole of its skin, which lay crumpled in a heap upon the ground. And in its place, grinning brazenly, stood none other than Kichapi!

'You!' she exclaimed. 'How did you . . .? You've been playing tricks on me! How dare you!'

'But my dear Gumiloh, I promise it wasn't my own idea to dress as an orang-utan,' said Kichapi politely. 'It was the fault of old Grandmother Kilimayuh.'

'Oh yes? And who is she? No doubt you'll be claiming that she's a witch.'

'Exactly right!' beamed Kichapi. 'She lives in another corner of the forest that you've never been to. The giants told me to stop off at her house on my way back to visit you. I had no idea what would happen. I passed the night there peacefully enough, but as soon as I woke up in the morning, the old hag grabbed me, chopped me up and threw me into her cooking pot! I bubbled and boiled inside there for hours. She skimmed off all the bad bits of me, Gumiloh, and threw them all away. Then she stuck the rest together again to make me perfect. Here I am now, just as she made me. See how handsome I am! Believe me, I am full of nothing but goodness. You can't refuse to marry me now!'

'Who are you to tell me who I should marry?' retorted Gumiloh.

'Oh, of course you must choose your husband of your own free will,' agreed Kichapi. 'But remember, Gumiloh, you have already shown me a great deal of affection when you believed I was your pet orang-utan. Think how hurtful it would be to reject me now.'

'I'd prefer any wild animal to you!' said Gumiloh haughtily.

'Oh, don't worry, I'm not offended and I'm not in the least disappointed,' said Kichapi. 'I know I'll win you in the end. Singiyang Naga himself has promised me that.'

'He has? And who on earth is he?'

'Goodness, haven't you heard of him? He is the chief of all the dragon-people that live at the bottom of the forest pools,' said Kichapi. 'He is a very dangerous being.'

'Dragon-people indeed!'

'Well,' said Kichapi, 'it's easy to be sceptical of such things when you lack the courage to visit the dark secret recesses of the forest. But remember, *I* am afraid of nothing. As soon as I discovered the way to his forbidden land, I dived straight to the bottom of the pool where it lay.'

Poor Gumiloh: she could not keep herself from asking: 'And what happened to you there?'

'Oh, Singiyang Naga tried to kill me many times. First he threw a spear at me: I caught it easily with my bare hands, and threw it back. Then, when I climbed the steps to his longhouse, he turned each one into the sharpest of knife-blades. Fortunately, however, I made friends with a firefly and the little thing lit a safe way up. Once I was inside, the chief tried to get me to sit on one of his poisoned mats – which I happen to know are specially designed to turn unwanted guests into ashes, so I crouched on the floor instead. When he offered me a drink of blood from all the previous visitors he had killed, I thanked him politely and secretly poured it away. That night he tried to stab me as I lay sleeping on the verandah; but he didn't realise that I'd stuffed my bed with bundles of rattan, and I was really hiding in the loft, watching him wasting his time.

'Well, the next morning, he was so amazed to find me alive and well that he gave me these three marvellous gifts. Look, here they are: a knife with a chipped blade, a bottle with a broken top, and a tiny fragment of tortoise shell.'

'Really!' exclaimed Gumiloh. 'What use is such rubbish to you?'

'They contain enough powerful magic,' Kichapi replied solemnly, 'to make me the happiest man on Earth. That's what I shall be, Gumiloh, when you marry me!'

'Oh, I've had enough of your tall stories, Kichapi! I tell you, the man I marry has to be genuinely brave: he has to prove it. I shall give you a single chance. Tomorrow my fiancé, Bilantur, is leading a war-party to a neighbouring village. They are going to take revenge on the people who murdered my father.

'If you are really such a superman, I expect you to join the raid. You must build yourself a war-canoe instantly; you must reach this other village before Bilantur; you must kill more enemies than he does; *and* you must bring back the dead enemy heads to me as proof. Do that, Kichapi – and who knows, maybe I will think again about my future husband: perhaps I *might* even take your own marriage proposal more seriously . . .'

The next day Gumiloh watched Bilantur and his followers set off to wage war. There was no sign of Kichapi. She shrugged, and went off to organise the festival which would be held to celebrate the raiders' return.

By nightfall the air was rich with the scents of roasting pork and chicken, and rice cooking in leaves of bamboo. Gongs were ringing, all the women were merrily dancing, and the priests and priestesses were busy making offerings to the ancestors and demons.

Gumiloh stood and waited. At last she heard the shouts of men coming up from the river. Then here they came, with her fiancé Bilantur leading the way.

'Gumiloh, my beloved,' he cried. 'Victory! See, I have brought you back two heads.'

But before she could examine them, there came another shout. Kichapi burst out of the trees, pushing poor Bilantur aside.

'Don't waste time looking at his worthless heads,' he yelled. 'I tell you, Gumiloh, they are disgusting! One is already so old it's riddled with worms: he's stolen it or dug it up from somewhere, you can be sure. As for the other one – it's just the head of a good-for-nothing dog! But *my* trophies, on the other hand . . . Look, I have brought back six heads to show you, my lady – and each is that of a mighty warrior, freshly slain by my own bare hands.'

At this, the gongs and the dancing stopped: the whole village fell silent.

'Tell me Kichapi,' said Gumiloh, 'and tell me the truth. How did you manage this, when this morning you hadn't even started to make a canoe to sail down the river in?'

'Oh, the canoe was a simple matter,' he replied. 'I just went into the forest and asked all the trees which of them wanted to become my boat. Very soon I saw one dancing with joy at the idea, so at once I cut it down. Then I called upon the wild creatures to help me, and straight away they came out of the undergrowth, *thousands* of them. The birds and insects had the tree hollowed out in no time. The monkeys painted it, and the bears and orang-utans dragged it down to the water. They worked so fast that I had time to share a quick feast with them all before I set off down the river.

'It didn't take me long to catch up with poor old Bilantur here, for he was stuck behind a terrible blockage on the water. It was full of logs, and clumps of bamboo shooting out like spears, and great boulders clapping together. I'm afraid your fiancé didn't have a clue what to do, but *I* soon shifted the lot just by singing a few of the magic songs taught to me by fierce old Singiyang Naga.

'After that, we all came at last to the enemy village. Bilantur had a few more hold-ups there – an evil water-demon tried to chase him out and so on – but I just rushed straight through everything with all my supernatural powers. Then I got one of my firefly friends to show me the way to the fellow who killed your father. By the time Bilantur finally caught me up, I'd slain the culprit and his five brothers, all with a single throw of my spear. Old Bilantur scratched around here and there, and eventually managed to find those two mangy old heads in an attempt to win your favour; but you'll have to agree they're not a patch on what I've done and brought. And after what you said yesterday, you'll *have* to marry me instead of him now, won't you?!'

Gumiloh laughed. 'I don't believe a word of what you tell me, Kichapi; but if your deeds are even half as great as your stories, I dare say I could be happy to make you my husband!'

So she did; and she was; and they lived together in peace and laughter for the rest of their days.

# Never Laugh at Animals

Dayak/Murut/Dusan,
Malaysian Borneo

Animals? They have their place, same as we do. Oh no, no one round here ever gets sentimental about them: not at all. I mean, chickens and pigs: they're just good for food; any dog in the village has to work for its scraps; and as for the forest animals, some we hunt, mostly we just leave them alone.

Yes, it's fine with us to kill just about any creature. Everyone shouts at their dogs, and there's plenty I know that regularly hit them. These things are perfectly okay, perfectly safe . . .

But there's one thing we all agree you should never do – and that is to *laugh* at an animal.

1

There was once a village not far from here at Mentu Tapuh, where a stranger came visiting, and he had his hunting dog with him. This fellow wanted feeding and a bed for the night, and straight away one of the men came forward and offered to look after him.

Well, the stranger was a bit of a show-off, and full of criticisms. He didn't like this, and he didn't like that. You know how it is: his hostess didn't handle her cooking pot as well as his own wife did; the sleeping mat they offered him was lumpy; the broken steps up to the longhouse were a disgrace; and so on.

Maybe some people would have sent him on his way, but our host and hostess were of a different kind. They decided to get their own back on the ungrateful wretch with a practical joke.

The lady of the household cooked a nice pork stew with rice for dinner. But when she served the stranger's plate, instead of his helping of meat, into the rich gravy she stirred some lumps of solid rubber!

Well, the family sat down to eat with the visitor. They were all watching him and hardly able to keep a straight face. But they'd reckoned without his dog.

Before the poor fellow could take a single mouthful, this
dog leaped up and snatched a meaty lump of rubber from his
plate. The next minute it was jumping around, making the most
extraordinary noises – it was trying to yelp, it was trying to
whimper – but for the life of it, it couldn't open its mouth to
do either, because its teeth were stuck fast together in the rubber!

Well, they knew it was dangerous . . . but the family had been
anticipating what would happen for so long that they just couldn't
keep the merriment inside of them. They all let go and laughed
and laughed until the tears ran and their stomachs ached . . .

The very next moment, they heard the wind roaring up outside.
Seconds later the wind had turned into a storm. Within the hour,
the storm had destroyed the whole village. And all the people
who were there at that moment were turned into stone.

2

Long ago, on this part of the River Pahl there used to be a big
longhouse, and one day the people decided to hold a grand feast.
It was a great occasion, and the festivities went on long after it
was dark.

Quite late in the evening, one of the men heard a woman's
voice calling across from the other side of the river shallows.

'What do you want, friend?' he replied. 'Are you coming to
join us?'

'I'd like to, but I'm scared to wade across in the dark in case
I slip. Can you fetch me a light so I can see where I'm going?'

'Wait there a few moments,' said the man; and he went off
to find if anyone could suggest how to light the woman's way
without getting their own feet wet.

Very soon, another man came up with a brilliant idea. It was
so original that everyone came crowding down to the river bank
to see if it would work.

He caught hold of a chicken and carefully tied a burning torch to one of its legs. Then he hurled it right across the water to the waiting woman, shouting:

'Here comes your light!'

The chicken went fluttering into the air with a terrified squawk. For a few moments the flames it carried lit up the night like a miniature sun.

But it was only half-way across when the flame burnt to the stick's end and the poor bird's feathers caught alight. With a shriek of pain, it crashed into the water and drowned.

As it dropped, everyone who was watching burst out laughing. The fools! Almost instantly, every single one of them was turned into stone.

3

See that pool there? It's a good watering hole: never runs dry. It didn't used to be there: it was formed many, many years ago when there was a different village here at Tiong.

The village headman at that time, he used to be a bit of a joker. He liked his rice-wine too. Anyway, one day he held this feast and got stupidly drunk. He had this dog he was quite fond of, and being in a crazy mood, he dressed it up in his little daughter's sarong; then he grabbed its front paws and started dancing all round the verandah with it.

Everyone else was just falling about with laughter, the dog looked so funny . . .

Idiots! The next minute it started raining; and the rain didn't stop until the whole village was flooded and lost under this pool.

Pig Power, Python Power

Lae district, Papua New Guinea

Come, share the feast! Now, how do you like the taste of this? It's snake meat: python. Yes, it's an old tradition here, to eat such meat. I'll tell you why, and how it came about.

Long ago, there was an evil sorcerer called Tagu. You see that tall, steep hill overlooking the village? That's where he used to live, right on top. Our ancestors lived in his shadow: in the shadow of his spells. Such dark, unspeakable things he tried to do to them! Within a short time, they would all have wasted away in the flood of his wickedness; but there was one thing that saved them: their pigs.

You know all about our pigs, of course: you understand how important they are to us? They are the whole measure of our wealth and well-being. Well, to our ancestors they were even more important, for their very flesh was imbued with magic. Its power was stronger even than Tagu's. Whenever they heard the evil one chanting up there, whenever they felt his spells coming down at them, the ancestors needed to do no more than eat some pig-meat. It gave them enough strength to deflect the evil, as a shield deflects a spear.

Tagu was angry: of course he was! He longed to wound our ancestors with his magic; he was hungry to tear them apart. He could not understand why he always failed.

Things went on like this for a long, long time, balanced dangerously.

Then one day a man from the village went out fishing, to a pool that lay directly under the sheer side of Tagu's hill. While he was there, a stranger suddenly appeared from the trees.

He was very small, this man: no bigger than a child. On his back he carried a basket woven from coconut leaves, held securely in place with many strong straps.

'Where have you come from, stranger?' asked the villager.

'I come from Tagu's hill,' replied the other.

'What! Then you must be in league with the sorcerer!'

'Oh no, not I,' replied the stranger. 'None of my people are. Oh, it's true that the foul one is our neighbour, but we try to have nothing to do with him, and he can't touch us with his evil.'

'How's that?'

The stranger patted his basket. 'Inside here each of us always carries secret medicines and herbs. Their power is stronger than Tagu's. So long as we keep these with us, we are always completely safe.' He stared up at the villager. 'So, fisherman, I have told you my people's most precious secret. If you have any honour, in return you will tell me yours. How do *your* people keep safe from the sorcerer?'

He was a fool, that ancestor of ours: honour is one thing, common caution is another. Straight away he told the stranger about the power of the pigs.

After that, the stranger went back up his hill. Who knows what went on up there in the thick forest, under the wet, swirling mist? Who knows if he shared his new knowledge with Tagu willingly – or whether the evil one forced him with unmentionable tortures to reveal his secret?

Anyway, the next day our ancestors woke up to find all their pigs were gone. And more: the village had suddenly become over-run with snakes!

What, are you afraid of them, slithering silently with their forked tongues? Our ancestors feared them too. Worse, they realised that this must be Tagu's work. Thanks to the stranger, he had discovered their secret and had used it to undo their protection against his magic.

They were angry! They prepared for war, to take revenge against the stranger and his people.

But before they could set out, weird things began to happen on the dark, misty hill-top. First they smelt smoke and heard sinister chanting. Then the air filled with screams that froze the blood . . .

Suddenly Tagu himself came hurtling down the hillside. The screams, the shrieks were his. The stranger's people had pushed him! At last he hit the bottom and flames flared up, heavy with the acrid odour of spells. And then – they saw that Tagu was no more: he was changed into a rock!

Look across there, at the bottom of the cliff: that huge boulder. That's him!

After his fall, the stranger's tribe came down the hill, bringing peace offerings.

'Listen,' said their chief. 'The snakes are really your old pigs, transformed by Tagu into new shapes. Eat them without fear, for their flesh contains protective powers even stronger than before.'

Since then, the stranger's tribe have always been our allies: we have never fought a battle against them.

We have new pigs now: see how they flourish around the village. And we have learned to love pythons, and eat them at every feast.

The Women's Revenge

Koitabu, Papua New Guinea

I don't know what it's like among your people – but here, it's us women who do most of the hard work.

Men! What are they good for? They spend half their time sitting round the fire, chewing betel nut and gossiping. Then, when they finally stir themselves to go hunting, they make such a fuss as if no one had ever killed a wild pig or wallaby before.

Not like us. We're up with the dawn each morning, tending our gardens – not to mention all the work we do, cooking, fetching water, looking after the little children. I was married at an early age – and I haven't had a day's rest since. Oh, I can tell you, the first time I heard the story of the bat-women, I wanted to run right away and join them!

Long ago in the time of the ancestors, the men got lazier than ever. They still went hunting from time to time – but they never brought a single piece of meat home. Instead they gorged themselves on the kill just where they caught it in the middle of the forest – and then had the cheek to go back to the village empty handed.

Well, the women thought something terrible must have happened, to drive all the game animals away. That was the lie the men spread about. Meanwhile the women carried on slaving away in the gardens, trying desperately to grow enough vegetables and fruit to fill the stomachs that were really crying out for meat.

They got pitifully thin; and as for the children, they were wasting away. What child can grow or even survive with nothing but bananas and yams to eat?

But the men were fit and strong as ever. Don't ask me how they could carry on like this. How could they watch their own little ones crying with hunger? How could they bear to see their wives so pinched and weak, even the ones that were growing big with child?

At last, on a day when the men were all away, the chief's wife called all the women in the village to a meeting.

'Listen,' she cried, 'I believe our husbands are all deceiving us. Where do they keep slinking off to so secretly? Why aren't they growing weak like we are? I've got my suspicions: but first, does anyone really know the truth?'

There was a long silence. Then a woman called Au stood up. They say she was young and newly married, and that tears shone in her eyes.

'I can tell you what is going on,' she whispered. 'My husband Gaigo: he's not like all the rest. He truly loves me. We have a baby coming: he wants it to grow strong. So every evening he comes home with a little meat hidden in his hair: he makes sure that I always get to eat it. He tells me in secret that this meat is left over from the men's feasting in the forest!'

At this a great ripple of anger spread through the women.

'Right!' commanded the chief's wife. 'The time has come for revenge, my sisters. Forget your work in the gardens today: instead come into the forest, away from the paths our husbands take. Today it is our turn to go hunting. Our quarry is this: a thousand magic black feathers.'

The women followed where she led them. They gathered many, many feathers.

That evening there was nothing to eat at all: no meat, no vegetables, no fruit, for the women had neglected their usual work. The men were angry: they screamed at their wives for being lazy. The women just shrugged and walked away, following the men's own habit. As for the children, they just curled up around their hunger pains and fell asleep.

The next day when the men were away, all the women came together again, bringing their feathers. The chief's wife showed how to sew them together. Then each woman tied a bundle to her arms.

Wings!

'Come,' cried the chief's wife, 'fly with me to freedom! Those men can take care of themselves in future. Yes, and let them look after their own children too for a change!'

Then they all flapped their wings. At once they rose into the air; and at that moment they were transformed. Now they were no longer women, but bats!

The bat-women flew high, high over the trees. They looked down. They saw the smoke of cooking fires; they smelt meat roasting; they heard their husbands laughing and belching over their clandestine feast.

Now their anger knew no bounds. They swooped down at the men, hissing and spitting.

'Look what we've become! We're leaving you for ever. Go home to the village and feed your children before they die of hunger!'

Then they rose again and flew away, scattering to dark, secret hiding places.

The men went back to the village. There they found their children crying. Gentle Au was trying to comfort them. She alone had stayed behind, out of love for her husband who loved her.

After that the men learned to feed their children as they should. The children grew strong again, they grew up, they had children of their own. They told them this story! Au taught the girls how to do women's work in the gardens; and now every father taught his sons the law that the hunt must be shared.

Stolen Goods

Masin district, Indonesian New Guinea

When the world was young there stood in the forest a marvellous
Tree. It was so tall, its upper branches broke through the white
clouds and touched the sky. Its roots were so deep, they reached
down, down to the very heart of the Earth. Its leaves were
countless; its flowers so fragrant that all who caught their scent
became intoxicated; its fruits were sweeter than honey.

At this time, the people were split up into two big clans.
Each clan had been born from its own Ancestor, long, long ago.
The people of each clan lived separately, in their own way;
yet sometimes they came together, worked together and helped
each other. Often they exchanged brides.

There came a day when the two clans met and discussed the
marvellous Tree. There were stories and rumours that fantastic,
magic things might lie within it. At length they agreed to cut it
down to find out. They also agreed that whatever they found
inside it, good or bad, they would share.

They took their stone axes and began to hack at the trunk. It
was so huge, so strong, it took them many hours. Sunrise passed
through noon, then dusk came softly. But at last it was done and
the Tree crashed down.

At once a great flood of water came gushing out of it! This is
how the sea was born.

And floating in the sea were all manner of wonderful things.
There were metal pots, sparkling jewels, plastic toys, gleaming
bottles of glass. There were books and guns. There were strange,
unnatural foods and drinks. There were machines that moved,
made pictures and sounds, even ones that seemed to think.

When they saw these things that came from the heart of the
Tree, one clan held a magnificent festival to celebrate. They
roasted pigs, they danced, they sang their thanks to the spirits.

But the second clan had no time for feasts or celebration.
Instead, they floated the fallen Tree onto the sea that had flowed

out of it. They worked fast and furiously, hollowing it out into a canoe. They filled it with every single one of the marvellous goods. Then, without delaying for farewells, they climbed into it and sailed away.

This sea, the sea from the Tree, it was as vast as the sky. The clan that stole the goods sailed across it for many moons, for many years. At last they came to another world. They took all the wonderful things out of the canoe and kept them there.

Time passed. The clan that was left behind, our clan, forgot the Tree. They forgot the wonderful goods inside it. First the memory became less than a dream; then it was lost completely.

More time passed: countless years. Then suddenly, in the days of our grandparents, strange men came to our country. They came from across the sea in massive ships, each one more enormous than a hundred canoes. They came from the air, in flying machines of shining metal, each one bigger than a thousand birds. With them they brought extraordinary goods – strange objects of metal, plastic, paper and glass.

Our grandparents were astonished. The elders and wise ones searched long and deep inside their memories; they searched beyond that, into the memories and dreams of the long-dead ancestors. At last the story came back to them: they remembered the Tree.

You strangers who come from distant lands, from another world, burdened with all the curious things that you say you cannot live without – you are our lost relations! Long ago your ancestors and our ancestors exchanged brides. And once, when the world was young, your people and our people cut down a magic Tree together. And while our clan sang and danced our thanks, yours stole all the riches from it and sailed away.

Now you come among us again, poking about our forest, meddling, asserting yourselves, asking too many questions.

When will you return the share of the riches that is rightfully ours? What must we do to get them back? Have we been patient for too long?

Sources

South America

Bunyard, Peter *The Colombian Amazon* Bodmin, Cornwall: The Ecological Press, 1990

Fock, Niels *Waiwai: Religion and Society of an Amazonian Tribe* Copenhagen: The National Museum, 1963

Hanbury-Tenison, Robin *Aborigines of the Amazon Rain Forest – The Yanomami* Amsterdam: Time-Life Books, 1982

Reichel-Dolmatoff, G. *The Shaman and the Jaguar* Philadelphia: Temple University Press, 1975

Villas Boas, Orlando and Claudio *Xingu: The Indians, Their Myths*, trans. Susana Hertelendy Rudge, London: Souvenir Press, 1974

Africa

Boesch-Achermann, Hedwige and Boesch, Christophe "Forest Close-ups" in *BBC Wildlife* [January 1992] Bristol: Wildlife Publications Ltd

Campbell, Joseph *The Way of the Animal Powers* London: Times Books, 1984

Knappert, Jan *Myths and Legends of the Congo* London/Nairobi: Heinemann Educational Books, 1971

Parrinder, Geoffrey *African Mythology* London: Hamlyn, 1982

Severin, Timothy *Vanishing Primitive Man* New York: American Heritage Publishing Co., 1973

Turnbull, Colin M. *The Forest People* London: Chatto and Windus, 1961

South-East Asia

Geddes, W.R. *Nine Dayak Nights* Melbourne: Oxford University Press, 1957

Jensen, Erik *The Iban and their Religion* Oxford: Oxford University Press, 1974

Poignant, Roslyn *Oceanic Mythology* London: Hamlyn, 1967

Rutter, Owen *The Pagans of North Borneo* Singapore: Oxford University Press, 1929/1985

Stokes, Donald S. and Wilson, Barbara Ker *The Turtle and the Island – Folk Tales from Papua New Guinea* Lane Cove, New South Wales: Hodder and Stoughton, 1978